THE ETHICS OF MARRIAGE

About the Author

HIRAM STERLING POMEROY, M. D., (Oren, Hiram, John, Noah, Joseph, Eltweed), b. Jan. 22, 1848, Somers, Conn.; studied medicine at Yale College, ill-health preventing the completion of the course; afterward studied in Germany and Austria, receiving the degree of M. D. at Leipsic; while studying in Europe he was connected with the missionary work of the American Board. He was a Fellow of the Massachusetts Medical Society; member of the Amer. Academy Pol. and Social Science, etc.; president of the Pomeroy Family Association, and a generous contributor to the expense for the investigation in England and Normandy. For his medical and surgical work, and for scientific writing he received the degree of M. A. from Yale in 1891.

THE ETHICS OF MARRIAGE

H. S. POMEROY, M.D

WITH A PREFATORY NOTE BY

THOMAS ADDIS EMMET, M.D., L.L.D

AND AN INTRODUCTION BY

REV. J. T. DURYEA, D.D

LOGOS PRESS
New Delhi-110 002

ISBN-13: 978-81-7268-232-3
ISBN-10: 81-7268-232-8

First Published 1820

Reprinted 2013

Printed and Published by

LOGOS PRESS

Building No. 4788-90, Street No. 23, Ansari Road,
Darya Ganj, **New Delhi**-110 002 (India)

Phone : 011-23272187 *Fax : 011-25357109*

Email: mail@logospressindia.com

Website : www.logospressindia.com

TO MY MOTHER

THIS LITTLE BOOK IS

AFFECTIONATELY AND REVERENTLY

DEDICATED

PREFACE

THE matters here treated have been on my mind and heart for many years. Heart-sickening facts have come to my notice within the past few months, and I feel it my duty to send out this warning in regard to what I consider the first and greatest danger of our family and national life. I believe the prevention or destruction of unborn human life to be, pre-eminently, *the* American sin, and that, if not checked, it will sooner or later be our calamity. This sin has its roots in a low and false idea of marriage on the part of some, and in others it is fostered by false standards of modesty.

On our statute books are excellent and ample laws bearing upon this crime, but public opinion is such that these laws are nearly a dead letter.

This appeal is made to the middle class-the rank and file of Americans-because they are the makers of public opinion, *and because they are, often unwittingly, the principal offenders.* It is understood that preachers find it easier and more agreeable to denounce the sins of other times, places, and castes than those to which they themselves belong ; how difficult and unpleasant a task it is to do the contrary I never before realized ; my courage has nearly failed me many times.

One may easily denounce the Mormons, because they are far away, and their peculiar sin is not shared by one's audience.

It is not a very difficult matter to work against intemperance, because the drunkard has little part in the moulding of popular sentiment ; but to use voice or pen in matters the free treatment of which must touch and grieve many whom one meets in the daily round of social and industrial relations, many even of those whom one holds near and dear, is not only a bitter and ungracious task, but also a most delicate one.

It was intended to give some statistics as to the spread of the evils touched upon, and to furnish more illustrations of them ; but it is almost impossible to obtain really trustworthy statistics, and the estimates made by medical professors and others who have referred to this crime are so appalling that the public is hardly prepared to receive them, and might derive more harm than benefit from seeing them in print. After carefully sifting the illustrations, there are but few left which may be used without grieving many who would see, or think they saw, themselves in the persons mentioned.

As these pages have been written there has crowded upon me a company of those who were *not* used as illustrations, and the number has grown until the sad and reproachful faces have haunted me like a nightmare.

While it has not been possible to treat this subject in such a way as to make the whole book suitable for reading aloud before a mixed company, yet there has been an honest endeavour to avoid that which might arouse or foster impure fancies, or offend a well-balanced judgment and refined taste. Some most excellent people will doubtless feel that it had been better to leave some points covered by the cloak which society, if not charity, throws over them ; but if such might have knowledge of all the facts possessed by the writer, there is little doubt that many of them would wish the matter probed more deeply still.

Others may feel that undue space is given to side questons, such as woman's work, home-making, the higher education of women, etc. All that concerns woman's education and employment has an important bearing, near or remote, on the question of maternity, and it is impossible to treat the sin against parenthood without touching upon what is called the Woman Question.

I am not a pessimist-quite the contrary. However doubtful the present may seem, I feel confident of the ultimate future ; whatever may be the sins and shortcomings of society to-day, I believe those of a century ago were graver andmore numerous.

A large share of the American sin is the result of ignorance of the laws of parenthood. I am so confident of the strength of character and the commonsense of the average American, that I am sure that very many of them will only need to be shown their mistakes in their theory and practice of marriage in order to set about correcting them. We Americans are an intense people ; if we surpass other peoples in some forms of foolishness and vice, we are at least teachable, and when we really undertake a reform, I believe we excel most others in the thoroughness of our work.

This little book can scarcely be said to have been written-it has simply grown. The first intention was to make a good-sized tract ; that grew into the dimensions of a pamphlet, and *that* finally developed into a little book, which has been written in odd moments from a busy life, much of the work having been done when head and hand were in need of rest ; furthermore, the author is a physician and not a writer, and this little book makes no pretensions to literary merit. There is also no attempt to exhaust the subject- this is simply a cry of warning, which is intended to set people to thinking and to bespeak their respect and attention for that which others will doubtless, in time, express to them by voice or pen much better than I could. It is earnestly hoped that this warning may reach many readers, and to this end the endeavour has been made to avoid wearisome statistics and the more purely scientific phases of the subject, which might not appeal to the average mind.

If these few pages may lend the smallest aid to the task of arousing popular interest in heredity as related to the family, and in the latter as related to the future of our country, they will have done their appointed work, and amply repaid the one who sent them forth.

241 Boylston St.,
Boston, December, 1886 **H. S. POMEROY**

CONTENTS

CHAPTER V.

CHAPTER VI.

CHAPTER VII.

CHAPTER VIII.

CHAPTER IX.

PREFATORY NOTE.

Professor Thomas Addis Emmet, M.D., L.L.D., Surgeon to the Women's Hospital of the State of New York ; ex-President of the American Gynaecological Society and New York Obstetrical Society ; Honorary Fellow or Member of the Obstetrical Societies of Boston, Philadelphia, Louisville, Little Rock, Berlin, and Edinburgh, of the Medical Society of London, Medical Societies of the States of New York, New Jersey, and Connecticut, etc., in his "Principles and Practice of Gynaecology," third edition, 1884, pp. 24 and 25, says : If we could attain this perfect physical development, might we not hope the marriage state would become more exalted with our people, among whom divorce is no rife, and nearer the bond which the Almighty evidently intended should exist ? Is it not our only hope that women may thus be rendered better fitted and more willing to accept the duties of maternity ? The healthy instincts of nature would then gradually wean back the hosts of women who have degraded themselves in their marriage relation, and have rendered what should have been a righteous mission a state of constant sin against the laws of nature. With due respect for decency, we can only refer to the various means employed to prevent conception, and to the frightful frequency of the practice of criminal abortion. Can any one accustomed to treating the diseases of women say in truth the statement is exaggerated that we see on any one day more sorrow and misery resulting from the abuse of the marriage state than would be found in a month from uncomplicated childbearing ? No one escapes, for sooner or later Nature will exact a grievous penalty for every violation of her laws.

"There lies a great missionary field throughout our land, and one in which only the medical profession can accomplish anything toward bringing about a healthier moral tone in regard to the marital state, and it is equally applicable to both man and wife. But before we can exercise the full influence we shall have to purify our own ranks, for we have many wolves in sheep's clothing among us. If the testimony of the sufferers is to be accepted, it is evident that we have more abortionists in the profession than out of it. Moreover, there are too many who, through ignorance of the consequence or from indifference, yield a quasi consent to, and sometimes even recommend the employment of, means to prevent conception.

"As a profession, we shall be judged derelict if we do not instruct the masses in regard to these matters, and in the proper mode of educating the females of the coming generation."

This matter was not in the previous editions of the book, and I was not aware of its existence until a few weeks ago, when, in conversation with him, I learned of his interest in the subject, and spoke of the book I had just written. Dr. Emmet at once referred me to what I have above quoted as expressing his views on this delicate and important subject.

I begged that he would read some parts of my manuscript and make some expression in regard to its pertinence and propriety. I also requested that he would state the position of our Catholic population in regard to the sins which I had touched upon.

In reply I received the following letter, which, the personal portions being omitted, I have his permission to insert here.

"89 MADISON AVENUE, N. Y.,
June 8, 1887.

"DEAR SIR : I have gone over your manuscript from beginning to the end, and particularly the chapters designated by you.

"You have stated the case in as strong terms as could be done in a work written chiefly for the public. I sincerely hope that it may bring forth good fruit, but I have my doubts. Those who take means to prevent conception, or who seek the aid of the abortionsit, are not, as a rule, ignorant, but they are indifferent as to all religious obligation. I have been in practice over thirty-six years, and for twenty-six years it has been devoted entirely to the treatment of the diseases peculiar to women. As a result of this experience, I can in all truth state the fact that these sins are not committed by the Jews or Catholics. I cannot recall a single instance of either practice where the individual lived up to her belief; so long as she was what the Catholics term 'practical' in practice they were pure. Every Jew and every Catholic is taught the duties of married life. Each child born is accepted as an additional evidence of God's especial favour. The Catholic is taught to regard marriage as one of the sacraments, and the slightest deviation from all pertaining to such a belief is a mortal sin....

"I honestly wish you success in your crusade against these sins of the people, but nothing can be accomplished unless you have the aid of the Protestant clergymen. They must take the nest generation in hand and sow the seed deeper, for only through the love of God can these sins be removed, or, rather, it will be the only safeguard against the practice ; with the present generation, I fear nothing can be done.

"Yours truly,

"THOMAS ADDIS EMMET.

" Dr. H. S. Pomeroy, Boston, Mass."

INTRODUCTION

In order that this book may be read with benefit, it will be necessary for the reader to understand and appreciate the aim and motives of the author. This cannot be said of all books, though it must be said of some, and said with emphasis of a few. The special reason in this instance will be presented. The subjects herein treated are seldom discussed even in conversation, rarely with earnestness, thoroughness, and completeness by voice or pen, never in presence of a mixed audience or on pages intended for ordinary readers. Among refined people, at least, the matters involved are reserved for private investigation and reflection. And inasmuch as sources of knowledge and methods of research are not open and familiar to many, and silence is preserved concerning them, they fail to be considered, and the results are error, vice, and often crime, and consequent injury and misery. Among men of intellectual and moral culture it is commonly supposed to be mark of delicacy not to refer to the topics of this treatise without a special occasion and a serious reason ; among women of the same kind and degree of culture it is deemed to be a mark of true modesty. Between men and women of this class they are never mooted.

To such persons it may be said, there is occasion and there are many serious reasons for a candid, careful, and complete consideration of these matters always, and especially at the present time. The reasons are such as to require the surrender of reserve and the breach of reticence. And this need not impair the purity of a true refinement nor the delicacy of a true modesty. This book may be an aid to the formation of a right judgment, a guide to correct practice, a help to the exertion of a salutary influence upon those who in ignorance and error sadly need to be enlightened and directed. It is published ; but nevertheless may be regarded as a private communication. It can be read in solitude, it can be passed to the hands of those who may peruse it alone.

It is admitted that, under present conditions, because of the notions and habits which prevail among us, it is difficult to treat such subjects with plainness and fulness. It must be conceded that it is impossible to do this without incurring criticism and censure. Nevertheless the exigency may demand the courage and fidelity which do not shrink from popular judgment, and even condemnation. There should, indeed, be no challenge given to criticism, nor any careless disregard of common opinion and feeling. The spirit and form of the treatise should be calm, refined, and judicious, even if it must be earnest and intense.

It is worthwhile, however, to inquire how it has come to be true that matters which are so central in your physical life, so essential in their relation to the condition, character, career, and destiny of every individual, so fundamental and vital to every institution and interest of society, cannot be " even so much as named among us." This fact alone is one of the most significant among the many indications that human nature has been strangely inverted and foully corrupted. But yet another fact remains. Veil these matters from our eyes as we may, they stare upon us in their manifest consequences. They are thrust on us constantly in our streets. We can scarcely unfold a single page of our public journal but they glare upon us.

To a very large number of those who commonly make objection to works of this order, of public addresses on these topics, as indelicate, if not impure, it is not important to make an explanation, much less an apology. They are too often moved by prejudice and sentiment, the latter as irrational as the former. This is evident from their lack of consistency. Every thorough teacher of righteousness who has been pressed by a conviction of duty to refer with severe cautiousness to these topics in public assemblies has learned of expressions of opinion and feeling not complimentary to his judgment and taste. Yet he has been able to discover that among his least lenient judges are men who do not always obey the precept, "Let no filthy communication proceed out of your mouth ;" women who are familiar with a certain sort of French romances ; men and women who sit together before the stage, on which the actresses appear certainly not "clothed," if they are "in their right mind." They are forced to think that there may be a form of modesty which is really spurious, and that fault-finding may be retaliation for fault found and set forth to the wounding of the heart through the conscience.

There may be many who will think the author impertinent in addressing them on such matters. Let it be remembered by them that he aims to enlighten their ignorance, correct their mistakes, save them from crime, warn them of peril, and rescue them, and others through them, from physical and moral injury and suffering. They have their protection. They are not compelled to read what he has written. It is now generally concede that one of the inalienable rights of man is "the liberty of prophesying." All profound moralists affirm that it is not only the privilege but the duty of a man who knows what others do not know, yet need to know, to teach them; who sees the wrong they do not see, and yet commit, to correct them ; who perceives the peril they do not discern, yet rush upon, to warn them : who anticipates the ruin they do not forecast, yet surely go to meet, to save them. Woe to him if he shuns the duty ! In the end the sting of a just conscience, the condemnation of just men, and the judgment of a just God will find him.

According to the ethical principles accepted by the medical societies, every physician is required to make known any remedy he may have discovered or applied successfully, and is expelled if he does not. Why ? Plainly because it is the duty of the members of the profession to relieve suffering, preserve and prolong life. According to the same principles, is it not the duty of the physician to disclose the tendencies of certain practices to cause suffering, shorten and terminate life?

It is commonly expected of physicians by their patients that they shall give instruction and directions in respect to general hygiene. It is expected of them by the community that they shall give information and counsel concerning sanitary measures and appliances. The motive is a desire for the preservation of health. It is clear, then, that commonsense affirms the duty of the physician to prevent as well as cure disease, or assist nature to effect the cure. The depth of the conviction from which this affirmation proceeds is evident from the fact that it is made notwithstanding it appears to require the practitioner to reduce his practice, the labourer to forego his occupation. But we have come to understand that an occupation is a service, and is primarily for the benefit of those who are served, and not of him who serves. Yet "the good and faithful servant" has his reward, first in his service, and then for it. Certainly he must have bread, and in the long run he will get it. Even in this world, which is supposed to have gone awry, the true man is sooner or later understood, appreciated, and fairly rewarded. His "bread and water are sure." If occasionally it is true that the faithful man must meet and bear popular prejudice and passion while withstanding the people for their good, and they threaten to keep back his bread, well, then, "it is written, man shall not live by bread alone."

If, then, it is allowed to be the duty of the physician to direct us in the care and use of our bodily powers, in order to the preservation and support of health and vigour, it certainly must be implied that he shall give us directions concerning the most fundamental of these powers—namely, the reproductive. If any one does not know and is willing to know-how central these are in the economy of the body, let him read a simple elementary treatise on biology. He should carefully note all that is taught about the principales of classification. When he finds that these are natural and not arbitarary, discovered and not invented, and that they are obtained from careful observation of all the organs of the body, in all their relations, functions, sympathies, and harmonies, he will be prepared to appreciate the significance of these in connection with the defence and maintenance of life and vigour. If classification proceeds upon the most essential likenesses, and these are most intimately associated with the operations of the organism as a whole, and are the peculiarities of the generative organs, then it is very evident that there must be the utmost peril to health and vigour in abuses of these, and the absolute conditions of the preservation of health and promotion of vigour must be a jealous care and normal use of them as indicated by their end and aim in the individual and the race. If it be conceded that several organs of the body have primary and also secondary ends, the latter pertaining to the social life of the individual, so that there may be more than one use for them, still it is true that the secondary must never supersede, much less defeat the primary.

On general principles, we commonly affirm that it is not safe to defeat the course of nature. On physiological principles inductively established, we must affirm that it is extremely dangerous. In view of the facts of clinical observation, we are bound to affirm that it is, at least by most methods, critically injurious. The guardians of the life and health of the people ought to tell them this.

The author is a physician and surgeon in general and special practice. He has had the advantages of training in a College of Arts, and all the helps to a thorough equipment for the functions of his profession. He has studied anatomy, physiology, hygiene, pathology, materia medica, surgery, etc., in the medical departments of two universities in this country and in Europe. He has had experience in domestic and hospital service at home and abroad. He is a specialist in knowledge and skill in the treatment of disorders of the organs to which reference is made in this work. He in now engaged in constant and varied practice. He knows the facts he adduces. He knows the habits of multitudes, and either observes or learns the consequences. He has been led to inquire extensively of other practitioners that he might gather other facts of the same order, to which he might refer in a published work without the possibility of enabling any reader to trace or even suspect their connection with persons. His confidential relations have made this precaution necessary. Where it has been practicable, he has made use of facts within the sphere of his own observation. Seeing that he has been in service in many places, and on two widely separated continents, it is not within the province of the reader to attach any example cited to and given individual.

The physician has not merely a professional relation to these matters. He cannot divest himself of his manhood, but must conduct himself in all his relations according to the demands of all its elements. He is bound by the moral law, and is a neighbour and a citizen, and must have a concern for the moral health of the individual and the community. No institutions are more fundamental to this than marriage and the family, and the integrity of the latter is dependent on the completeness of the former.

The family is the first and most essential school for the education and training of the young into all the qualities of a perfect manhood, the general and special preparation for the fulfilment of the duties and enjoyment of the privileges which are implied in the various relations of our complex life. Marriage is necessary to the existence of the family and the attainment of its moral ends. A true marriage, truly fulfilled, is necessary to the perfect family and its effectiveness for its moral functions. Whatever impairs the integrity of marriage mars the family and defeats its objects. Animals may not mate, or they may mate temporarily ; or when the care of both parents is necessary to offspring, they do mate and provide the nurture.

For reproduction, men need not mate. For the care of offspring, they must. And for the proper care of intellectual and moral offspring they must mate permanently. This is the judgment of the civilized world, and needs not to be reconsidered. Some things are settled in this late period of the experience of the best portion of our race.

Those, then, who are not willing to become parents ought not to marry. Those who are not willing to consecrate marriage to the family, and the family to its high ends, ought not to marry.

It is conceded, in view of the various elements of human nature, that marriage may have other ends than the propagation of offspring, and the education of moral persons for private and public life and its relations may afford the means for the attainment of those ends. But the incidental issues of an institution are surely compatible with its primary intention, and should be sought in connection with and mainly through the accomplishment of that. Those who cannot enter into a completely congenial marriage, and therfore refuse to accept one imperfect of revolting, must substitute for it such pure relations as are analogous in their effects on character and the conduct of life. Those who are incapable of bearing children must supplement their imperfect state by similar relations. The exceptional, however, furnishes no criterion for the general and normal.

To enter marriage with a purpose to defeat its primary end is to violate it. Those who pervert it inevitably degrade themselves. They sink from the plane of an intellectural and spiritual relation into a connection beneath their nature as a whole. They surrender to a part which is the humblest, and which out of its proper adjustment to the noblest not only becomes the lowest, but ceases to be human at all, and lapses into the purely animal. So long as the aim is upward the whole nature is elevated. This is true even when there is a physical bar to the accomplishment of the intended aim.

If the desire be to avoid offspring, nevertheless, the purpose is not always effective. The result is, that parentage is not intentional when it occurs. According to the principles of heredity, so far as they are at present understood, it would seem that this must tend to incompleteness of offspring. It is well known that the mental state of parents modifies the condition of childern, physical, mental, and moral. An infant born under such a mental state as repugnance to offspring in the parent is to be pitied. It is almost as forlorn as an orphan. Well is it that nature has implanted instincts in those who are "without natural affection," otherwise it would go hard with the poor little waifs, the "creatures of accident," in too literal a sense. The struggle of life, as life now is, is surely hard enough to accept without the added calamity of such an introducation to it.

The statesman and patriot has much to make him anxious for the future welfare of communities. The persons who have the material and intellectual resources for the best service in rearing childern and fitting them for society and citizenship are more and more neglecting the duty. Those who have the benefit of a good mental and moral inheritance are not bequeathing it. Others are multiplying. The majority soon will take possession with its evil heritage. Heredity will work against the spiritual forces which are striving to elevate and bless the individual, the nation, and the race.

Religious people have especial need to consider these things. Piety may not be inherited, but it is favoured by many elements and tendencies of our nature which are inherited. The organized agencies for the religious instruction and culture of mankind have not usually been composed and energized by those who are incorporated from without, but developed from within. The family is the source of the Church, and enters it as a unit of its life, a solid factor in its organism. For this reason all teachers of religion should manifest their cordial sympathy and give their hearty support to the sociologists who are endeavouring to secure the integrity and purity of marriage, to devote it to the family, and so conserve its high ends, and accordingly aim to instruct and guide, to caution and warn, the people in respect of the uses and abuses of these fundamental and sacred institutions.

JOSEPH T. DURYEA.

CHAPTER I.
THE FAMILY AND THE STATE.

THE ETHICS OF MARRIAGE.

CHAPTER I.

THE FAMILY AND THE STATE.

THE production and preservation of the individual is the common task of the family and the State. In this responsibility they are something more than mere partners, for in a numerous and complex society like ours of to-day, each is absolutely dependent upon the other. The production and preservation of the individual is not simply their responsibility, it is their first and greatest one. They are also vitally interested in the cultivation of the individual ; but in order to his satisfactory cultivation, he must be well born, and his early years must be guarded as only the family and the State, working together, can guard them.

It would seem like a waste of words to multiply them in the effort to prove the mutual dependence of the family and the State, and yet each seems wofully ignorant of, or, at least, indifferent to its responsibility to the other.

The family cannot thrive except under the protection and help of the State, and the latter cannot exist except as the whole, of which the families are the parts.

On every side we hear complaints of the sins and shortcomings of the State. Those who find fault seem to forget that they are themselves a part of that of which they complain, and that the character of the whole is but the resultant of the character of the parts.

In a republic all civil reform must have its roots in reform of the individual and the family. Tracing a reform back to its source, we find that an officer of the law carries out the orders of the executive, the executive carries out the provisions of the law, the law is an expression of the will of the Legislature, the Legislature is elected by the voter, and the voter's will is usually the expression of his birth and home training. And so we may trace reform back to the nursery. I shall endeavor in these pages to show that reform may be traced still farther back, or, rather, that *preform* lies back of *reform*.

If all who have the right to help make the laws and secure their enforcement should have an interest in voting, and vote intelligently and conscientiously, all would be well, or, at least, vastly better than it is ; but this is not the case. Many of our most intelligent citizens seldom or never vote, and one political party might almost be called the Fair Weather Party, for it is almost sure of defeat in an election held on a stormy day. A New York physician boasted to me last year that he should not vote, but that he was *sure* his party would win. He did not vote. His party did not win, and it met defeat because he, and thousands of others like him, trusted that some one else would do for them that which they were unwilling to do for themselves. There recently came to my notice a case where there were seven voters in one house, and but two of them voted on election day. The other five might have voted if they had been provident, and had felt willing to make a small sacrifice of convenience to duty. There are two kinds of voters—those made by hand and those turned out by machinery. The former is liable not to vote at all, the latter is almost sure to vote once, and we are thankful if he does not vote "early and often" in the same election.

We can never have satisfactory laws which shall be vigorously executed until each home in the land becomes an institution for rearing and educating intelligent, conscientious voters who will be ashamed not to vote when it is possible to do so.

The indifferent citizen does the State a double wrong when he neglects to vote ; he fails to make good laws, and he fails to support them heartily when others have passed them ; for the non-voting citizen is usually a lukewarm growler, and feels but a half-hearted interest in laws which are not of his making.

I asked a very intelligent lawyer why it was that certain forms of crimes flourished while there were stringent laws for the punishment of them. His reply was substantially as follows : "Those laws never expressed public opinion, not even that of the Legislature which passed them. One or two legislators, it may be, had a conscientious desire for them ; they framed and introduced them, and their fellow-legislators, either through good nature voted for them or through indifference failed to oppose them. As those laws never represented the conscience and will of the public, they are practically a dead letter." Accordingly, conscience and will must lie behind the law, and birth and nursery training lie behind them, and so we are again brought back to the family as the source of civil order and prosperity.

It would seem as though the State would be the careful guardian of the family, yet these same dead-letter laws *—if it be proper to call that dead which never was alive—are intended to prevent the wholesale destruction of the embryo citizen, and the debasement of the whole family relation.

We are happy in that Church and State are separate ; we are unfortunate in that family and State are not enough united. They belong together, and neither can become prosperous and effective apart from the other. If the family neglect its duty to the State, it may be proper for the Church to stir the family up to its duty in this respect, because only as it bears its share of the burden of government can it hope to have the protection which the enforcement of wise laws alone can give.

It is a discredit to the intelligence and wisdom of the heads of families among what are called the better classes, that very few of them attend caucuses, and many of them seldom vote. No one has a right to complain of the laws or of their non-enforcement so long as he is neglecting his opportunity for helping to bring about a better state of things. It is foolish to say that the case is hopeless. There is enough virtue and manhood among the voters of this country to secure and enforce ample laws for the protec-

* See Appendix.

tion of the interests of our homes, if only the virtue and the manhood would take courage and combine for a common end.

Impure literature, coarse and debasing illustrations of still more coarse and debasing stories and items, "doctors'" signs which advertise to the initiated that, for a price, the healing art will be prostituted to the lowest ends, flourish in nearly all our cities and large villages. Our leading newspapers, many of them, at least, regularly print advertisements which are but thinly-disguised invitations to crime, and among a certain class of shops, which are supposed to bear a relation to the office of the Good Samaritan, it would probably be difficult to find one which did not deal in that which the law of the land and the laws of most of our States and Territories make it a penal offence to advertise or sell.*

* I referred to this in conversation with a very intelligent young man who is a clerk in one of these shops in a large village in one of our Middle States. He assured me that representative people, women as well as men, freely and unblushingly bought such articles at his store. He added that he did not believe the law of his State made such sale illegal. I find that this State has more stringent laws on this matter than any other State or Territory, *it being there a criminal offence to own such articles, even though they be not disposed of by sale or gift!* I attempted to gather some accurate statistics in regard to the illegal sale of such goods, but at the very outset I found so appalling

And last, but not least, it would be difficult to find a hamlet in the country or a street in a city where unborn children had not been destroyed by those who were bound by every law of God and man to cherish and protect them!

With the law nearly a dead letter, with the worse class of the medical profession arrayed on the side of evil and the better class of the profession mostly silent, with the press and the pulpit mostly following the priest and the Levite in passing by on the other side, and with the crime flourishing in places high in society and the Church, what can be done? Surely it is time that we realize the vital interests which are common to the family and the State, and the grave danger, if not disaster, which must await us if we long neglect them. If the family suffers from the neglect of the State, it is no less true and important that the State is imperilled by the neglect of the family. It is coming to the pass that our voters—and so our law-makers and rulers, indirectly, if not directly—come more and more from the lowest class, because that class is able and willing to have children, while the so-called better classes seem not to be.

---

a state of things that it seemed a waste of time and effort to push the investigation.

The fact that seven elevenths of the births in our immediate section are of Catholic origin is a sad comment upon Protestant civilization. It is but fair to say that the Catholic people and the lower classes are comparatively free from the crime of the destruction of unborn human life.

Perhaps, under the circumstances, the course taken by the pastor of one of our large and influential New England churches during a recent political campaign was justifiable.

He announced the usual weekly prayer-meeting, and added: "As a caucus of our section occurs at the same hour, of course we shall not expect the brethren to be present; I regret that I cannot myself go to the caucus." The day and hour for the two meetings arrived, and the usual brethren appeared in their usual places in the prayer-meeting. The pastor looked the audience over carefully, and then said: "I see the brethren have forgotten the caucus to-night; we will sing hymn No. — while they go out," and they went; probably it was the first time some of them had ever attended such a meeting.

Did the poet Pryor have a prophetic vision of American society of the nineteenth century when he wrote the words: " . . . fine by degrees, and beautifully less"? Certainly the words fit our case, for it is the rule, to which there are pitifully few exceptions, that as our families grow "fine" they also become "less." In fact, many of them are becoming extinct, and we are depending upon foreigners of every nationality, of every degree and of no degree, to fill up the gaps in our ranks. The gaps are becoming so many and so large that soon, if we do not bestir ourselves, the ranks of American national life will belong to them and not to us. If this ever comes to pass it will be strictly in the line of the divinely ordained principle of the survival of the fittest, and men and angels will say amen.

We frequently hear it spoken of with surprise and regret that when a family acquires wealth and culture, and is in a position to be the most useful, it should begin to decline, and its place be taken by those below it. When a family begins to decay it is already past its point of highest usefulness, and its removal is no mystery; it is but the penalty for the mental, moral, and physical sins of the family itself. It is no longer fit; it may no longer survive.

Mens sana in corpore sano, a sound mind in a sound body, is as true a saying now as when the words were first spoken. This is good morality as well as good philosophy. If not in the history of single individuals, yet in that of several generations, it is seen to be true that soul, mind, and body were intended by the Creator to be mutually helpful, and that if one suffer, the others must suffer with it. There are many false estimates current in society in regard to many things, and perhaps in respect to none more than in matters of the family.

We pride ourselves on our zeal for the sanctity of the family relation, and yet we entertain false and dangerous ideas respecting marriage; and these ideas are leading to practices which will, if unchecked, soon corrupt and destroy our national life. A healthy marriage begets a healthy family, and a sufficient number of healthy families beget a healthy State. So the ideal State may be traced back to true views and treatment of the marriage relation.

This may be objected to; it may be said that a State is but an association of individuals, and that the State really has little or nothing to do with the family, as such. This is not true; there could no more be a strong and symmetrical State created by single individuals than there could be a durable and convenient house built by throwing together a conglomerate mass of building materials. The State is dependent upon the family relation for the proper conditions for the generation of the individual; it looks to the family for the proper rearing of its youthful citizens, and, finally, the State depends upon the family relation to hold the mature citizen to prudent and safely conservative thought and action. The unmarried man is seldom so cautious, temperate, and reliable as he who, by becoming responsible for wife and children, has "given hostages to fortune," and shrinks from hasty or ill-advised action because it might harm others than himself.

Must it always remain true that in America wealth and prosperity of the family put a premium upon its decay? I believe not. Since the world was created it has probably been the rule that the overworked and underfed toiler who came into sudden wealth straightway took a holiday and made himself sick by self-indulgence; and the Newrich family has usually been ridiculous to others and dangerous to itself for a generation or two, while it was learning the proper use of its newly-acquired resources. We Americans are a sort of Newrich family in the society of nations. We have been poor and provident; we have grown rich and improvident. We have become wasteful, not only of all that is needful to the support of life in comfort, but we have become ruinously extravagant in the use of those mental and physical resources which are necessary for the proper transmission of life and the perpetuation of the race. Worse than this, in our mad effort to wring the last drop of present enjoyment, we have so forgotten ourselves, have stooped so low, as to destroy unborn human life!

In course of time, if the Newrich family do not commit suicide by self-indulgence and vice, nor join the ranks of the pauper class, it becomes used to its prosperity, grows conservative, and takes its place as a useful member of society.

There are some encouraging signs of the times indicating that we Americans are beginning to use wisely much of the wealth which we have hitherto abused, and that the family and the State are about to join hands in the effort to do more and better for each other than ever in the past.

And a little child shall lead them.

CHAPTER II.

MARRIAGE.

THE door to the family relation is marriage; the higher a people is in the scale of intelligence and morality, the more formal and binding will be its marriage tie, and the more jealously will it be guarded against all that might tend to weaken it. It follows naturally that, if there is to be the highest type of family, it must be founded upon correct and high ideals of marriage. If we confine our view to the civilized world, we are forced to conclude that the views and practices of the multitude are imperfect and below an ideal standard.

Strange to say, these have, to a degree, gained admittance through the guise of modesty and purity. The spirit of evil has at times wrought great devastation in the name of religion, and now it is working against purity in the name of purity itself.

Society declares that it is indelicate, even unsafe and impure, to speak of matters which have a divine Author and are instituted for an honorable and necessary end. Ostrich-like, society hides its head while the calamity comes upon it unawares.*

So it has come about that every possible reason, except the first and highest one, is given for marriage, and many marriages, in consequence, have in them every possible element except the most important one, and are like the play of "Hamlet" with the Hamlet left out. Convenience, policy, friendship, position, influence, money—all these are given as motives for matrimony, and in addition we have the ideal marriage of romance—that for love. Most marriages belong to one or more of these classes, and yet this list contains only the subordinate factors of a perfect marriage. If such a life union prove to be wise and prosperous, it is little praise to those most concerned, but is because a wise and kind Providence overrules the mistakes of ignorance and folly.

Let us look at truth as God made it, if we can ; let us "call a spade a spade"! It is time for us to stop insulting the Creator by assuming that some of His ordinances make the obedient dishonorable or immodest.

Marriage concerns others besides those who contract it, and only in the light of its bearing

* Let the reader consult any candid physician who has a large general practice.

upon the future welfare of those others can it be fairly estimated and safely undertaken.

True marriage is the life union of one man and one woman who are in suitable conditions of health in mind and body, of age, of temperament, of convictions, and of tastes to enable them to live together in harmony and happiness, to assist each other in fulfilling the general ends of human life in the development of character and performance of duty, *and to become the parents of healthy offspring;* marriage means just this, no more, no less. It means no more, because with these conditions every possible advantage of a prosperous and joyous marriage must follow as inevitably as the shadow follows the object ; it means no less, because with less it must be incomplete, and the incomplete always fails of all its ends. We imagine that our standards of modesty show our civilization and culture, but we are wrong. A genuine and high state of civilization and culture of the whole man would neither need nor demand such false codes of modesty ; indeed, these are really remnants of semi-barbarism. Some of the American aborigines had codes of modesty in respect to reproduction far more strict than ours, while Greece and Rome in the palmy days of their greatness and virtue were immodest if judged by our standards. The reader may think I take a low view of marriage; were man simply an animal it might be true, for then marriage would be simply a physical relation. But man has an intellect, a soul; and profound and sincere considerations of his genesis must involve the intellectual and moral nature as well as the physical; and a high ideal of marriage as primarily the means for the perpetuation of the race must necessarily carry with it a high ideal of marriage viewed in its broadest light, for the Creator has in this world so joined together the mental, moral, and physical factors that go to make the normal and complete human being, that we cannot safely separate one from another.

Were the subject of reproduction given the high, frank, and honorable recognition it deserves, our standard of real modesty and virtue would be raised, society would be saved from many loathsome and dangerous sins of ignorance, and a marked improvement in the whole man, mental, moral, and physical, would follow.

The Creator has, for wise ends, implanted certain instincts and passions in each member of the human family; as these instincts and passions are intimately connected with important ends, they have been made strong, and have been closely connected with the central organs and functions of the body and mind. They are invaluable servants, but bad masters. They must be judiciously directed and controlled, else harm and degradation are certain. Yet society declares that these same instincts and passions must be nearly or quite ignored during the period of their development, and referred to, if at all, in a shamefaced and apologetic way after their maturity. The result is that, more often than not, they are inordinate, and control the life which they should only serve.

The individual on the threshold of manhood or womanhood should be taught, earnestly and reverently, the laws and functions of the whole being as far as these are known to science; should be taught the meaning and aim of the reproductive instincts and passions, and the serious responsibilities they imply. It may be objected that this sort of instruction is largely beyond the comprehension of the boy or girl of ten or twelve, and, even if comprehended, would inflame the mind and work great mischief.

This is a mistake; the American boy or girl scarcely more than half the age referred to is capable of understanding, and often does understand, almost everything which should not be known about this matter. It certainly does seem a pity that the young person may not be spared the burden of knowledge of this sort for some years beyond the time indicated ; but this is seldom possible, for in various ways—from nature, from comrades, and from stories—children will learn about reproduction, and the information which comes to them in these ways piques curiosity and may inflame passion, but never properly instructs.

If these lessons are well learned in early life, they have a salutary influence during all after years, not only keeping the life more pure, but sparing the mind the burden of imaginary ills and woes.

If the secret history of those about us might be known, it would appear that many a person groans beneath a burden of delicacy, sensitiveness, and anxiety which are unnecessary and false, but which, having been assumed in childhood, cannot be thrown off, even though the mature judgment be aware of their real character. This is the brighter side of the picture. The darker side is black enough, but does not come within the province of this chapter. It is well to begin early, because, as already suggested, right ideas of marriage have their root in character, and must be planted in seed-time if we would have a harvest in its season. The New England farmer who should plant in July expecting to gather in August would be accounted insane, but he who sows seeds of character at nineteen expecting to find a harvest at twenty is often accounted wise. Rapidity of development is usually in inverse ratio to the value of the product; character is a slow grower.

Romance and the drama, while more sensible and pure than they were a half century ago, are yet largely to blame for the false idea of marriage. In the conventional novel or play the hero and heroine fall in love and—"live happily ever afterward." There may have been great disparity in condition and circumstance; one or the other may have been unfit for marriage under any circumstances; but that mysterious alchemist, Love, turns all dross to gold, makes all unfitness fit, and all is well! This is bad philosophy and bad morals. It is evil seed, and it brings forth an evil harvest of incompatible marriages and scandalous divorces, to say nothing of graver wrongs and even crimes.

That which seemed the most genuine love sometimes proves to have been but passion; yet even a strong and genuine love cannot effect impossibilities. It cannot make the small and narrow nature large and broad; it cannot make the feeble intellect strong, nor can it transform the drunkard or debauchee into one who has always had a sound and clean physique and is a really safe progenitor.

In arrangements for marriage the heart and the head should be in much the relation of the Senate and the House of Representatives. The heart should not seriously consider a matter which has not first approved itself to the judgment; nor, on the other hand, should any measure be passed over the veto of the heart. We look with horror on the marriage of convenience and policy so often made on the continent of Europe and elsewhere in the civilized world; but is it, after all, so much worse than many of our marriages for love when other considerations have been left out?

We lead the world in the matter of divorce. In nearly all cases the divorced believed, at one time, that they were sincerely in love. They appear to have been mistaken, and if they had carefully considered marriage in all its length and breadth, all its conditions and duties, their love would probably have failed them before marriage instead of after, and much sorrow and shame would have been spared to them and others.

It is not surprising that we have so many unfit and unhappy marriages. The wonder is, rather, that there are not many more of them when we consider the hap-hazard way in which they often come about.

The strength of character and the wonderful

adaptability of the American people are nowhere better displayed than in the fact that so many of these ill-advised marriages turn out fairly well. Persons of character and self-respect, seeing their mistake when it is too late to undo it, set to work to make the best of it; perhaps they have a life struggle to conceal their disappointment and pain, or it may be that they are able to adjust themselves to their unfavorable circumstances, and finally wring victory out of defeat.

Even at the best, such a marriage must be a partial failure. The elements of an ideal marriage are subtle, and success or defeat has an influence beyond the present, even into future generations. Many an unsuitable marriage which has been made the best of, and finally becomes fairly satisfactory to the husband and wife, has the history of its defeat written in the characters and lives of the children who were born under the unfavorable conditions.

Disguise the matter how we will, yet the fact remains that the first and specific object of marriage is the rearing of a family. We may never hope to have the marriage relation what it ought to be so long as social usage demands that we pretend it is for any or every object except the real one.

Marriage has secondary objects and compensations, such as the preservation of virtue, companionship, etc. The first of these is affirmed by Scripture, and we are justified in recognizing its importance; but there is grave danger of estimating it too highly, or, rather, of failing to give it any true estimate. The danger is that we confound means and ends. Physiologically considered, there can be but one end in marriage—the breeding and rearing of a family; but there are various means which conduce to this end by preserving the mental and physical tone and balance of husband and wife, and cultivating in them a union of regard and affection without which any mere outward union can be but a travesty of marriage. How far it may be proper to exercise the secondary objects of marriage, it is impossible to state in any general rule, because individual cases vary so greatly; but it is safe to say that the phase of marriage which is most closely allied to its primary object has an important bearing on the health, happiness, and harmony of husband and wife, and so may properly be exercised by those who have a proper regard for the primary end of marriage, even when its relation to this end be but indirect, provided such exercise of it be kept within the bounds of mental and physical health.

CHAPTER III.

THE PERVERSION OF MARRIAGE "THE AMERICAN SIN."

THE general observer has little idea how many and how bitter are the fruits of hasty and spurious marriages. Now and then he reads a newspaper account of some phase of conjugal infelicity, of a divorce, or a wife murder, and receives a vague impression that something must be wrong somewhere, and feebly wonders that somebody does not do something about it; this is too often the extent of his information and interest.

As the geologist may see a quarry cropping out at points where the casual observer supposed he saw but isolated rocks appearing above the surface, so the physician may see the marks of iniquity where others have noticed only slight follies and mistakes.

The physician must see these things whether he will or not, for those who do them are constantly presenting themselves to him and seeking his aid, both before and after the acts, and are usually willing to pay large fees for the service required. There is a very respectable number of the profession to whom the offer is no temptation whatever, but there are too many regularly educated and respected physicians who are willing to debase the healing art to infamous ends, provided there be care to maintain secrecy, some color of excuse, and the fee be large enough to make some amends for loss of self-respect. Besides this, our cities and large towns are overrun with quacks and charlatans, who fatten on the fruits of crime.* It is a disgrace to our Commonwealth that she allows them full liberty to carry on their nefarious work under the guise of the noble profession of medicine.

The fruit of ill-advised marriage in which society is just now the most interested is divorce ; but divorce is not the worst. That grade must be accorded to what our neighbors across the Atlantic call the American sin. I am not proud of the name. I would gladly substitute some other and less suggestive one, but I believe the name is a just reproach to us, and it may be for our future welfare if we meet it squarely now.

By the American sin our neighbors mean the destruction of unborn human life. We point

* The advertisement of one of these was left at my door as I was writing these words !

the finger of scorn at them because of the number of their illegitimate births. They reply that theirs is not a sin against nature, only a crime against society, and then they accuse us of both the sin against nature and crime against society—and we are dumb before their accusation.

It must not be supposed that the physician has the most trouble with those who belong to the lower classes. These give comparatively little trouble in this way. They seldom apply to the reputable physician, and when they do they are easily refused.

The real difficulty comes from so-called highly respectable people, even from leaders in social and religious movements. We never know when some one of these may not implore one of us, as a family physician, to do that which is a sin before the law of God and man ; and when to the entreaty there are added the tears and pleading of a charming woman, the situation becomes embarrassing and unpleasant in the extreme.

This seems an ungracious thing to say, especially as the physician is under peculiar and delicate bonds to respect the secrets of his patrons. But the time is already past when silence could be a virtue, and it seems as though the very stones would cry out if he does not give speedy warning of the danger which threatens our social life and health.

Even the physician is at times puzzled to know where patients could have obtained the information necessary to the commission of their crime. Investigation brings to light the fact that there is in our midst a school of instruction in the art of avoiding parenthood. This school carries its instruction to pupils in the most remote nooks of our land, and does its work so quietly and unobtrusively that a husband or wife may be enrolled in it without the other ever suspecting it. For convenience we will call it the blank school.

This institution has special advantages, inasmuch as a large part of its instruction is given by voluntary teachers, who are enthusiastic about the branches which they teach, who make most of their instruction personal and verbal, and who supplement the course with experiment and practice.

This school indignantly repels the idea that it is doing anything improper; indeed, it frequently makes the claim that it is serving the ends of human weal and progress.

The text-books and the recognized instructors of the blank school are not inviting to a pure and cultivated taste. The former consist mostly of newspaper advertisements which a respectable woman would prefer not to be seen reading, and of reports of lectures "to ladies only," etc., which are always printed at the expense of the lecturer.

The recognized instructors are mostly persons of no position in society, although some of them have medical diplomas and more or less social and professional standing. The public knows these persons by the name of abortionists.

But these means of instruction are not considered respectable in good society, and as a large share of the pupils in the blank school have good social positions, it follows that much of the instruction must be given in some less coarse and shocking way. As a matter of fact, many of those who have become adepts in the art of avoiding parenthood have never come in contact with these means of instruction, but have learned their lessons of some kind friend or neighbor, who taught as a labor of love, and stood ready to illustrate by experiment and assist the pupil in actual practice.

So dense is the general ignorance respecting the crime against parenthood—the loathsome and criminal character of it, I mean—that doubtless many who read this book will be surprised and shocked to learn that it is corrupting the vitality of society, and is a crime before the law. The prevention or destruction of unborn human life is, in America, verily the "terror that walketh in darkness and the destruction that wasteth at noonday."

So small a matter is it considered by many women that they look upon professional talent as quite unnecessary, and an abortionist as causing needless trouble and expense, and so they manage the affair themselves, using for the purpose various household instruments which it makes one shudder to think of, or endeavoring to accomplish the end by means of drugs. We meet in our practice women who would hesitate to harm a fly, but who admit to having destroyed a half dozen or more of their unborn children, speaking of it as they would of the drowning of superfluous kittens.

The institution for teaching the art of avoiding parenthood is a graded school. There are about a dozen classes in all, covering a wide range of instruction, extending from indifference to the duty and blessedness of parenthood to outright murder, which is the accomplishment taught in the last class.

There are so many classes that the step from one to another is a comparatively easy one. Many a one guilty of child murder began the course of crime by simply fostering the idea that children are unnecessary encumbrances.

The real beginning is in early life, when young people are taught, directly or by implication, that reproduction is a matter concerning which speech is indelicate, of which it is proper, even, to feel ashamed; as they grow older and the period of marriage draws near, they learn to look upon parenthood as a responsibility and a burden which they may properly avoid if possible.

They make their plans for marriage, although they have neither the inclination, health, nor means for rearing a family. Very likely the only recognition they make of the possibility of children as the result of marriage is to consult a physician as to the most safe and sure and convenient way to avoid parentage. It is surprising with what *sang froid* they will broach this matter, assuming at the outset that what they propose to do is quite proper and entirely feasible; they express surprise if the physician questions the morality of the proceeding, and are quite incredulous when he professes to doubt the possibility of it; and yet a tell-tale look in the eye and a suspicious flush on the cheek usually give the impression that they are compounding with self-respect.

In many cases these pupils in the blank school have carefully and persistently trained themselves for the step they are now taking by studying the writings of the disciples of Malthus, and have nearly or quite stilled the reproaches of conscience, just as the would-be murderer prepares himself for his crime by first getting under the influence of liquor.

It is surprising to what an extent the laity believe that medical science knows how to control the birth-rate. Just here let me say that I know of but one prescription which is both safe and sure,—namely, *that the sexes shall remain apart.* So thoroughly do I believe this to be a secret which Nature has kept to herself, that I should be inclined to question the ability or the honesty of any one professing to understand it so as to be able safely and surely to regulate the matter of reproduction for those living in wedlock.

Failing to obtain the desired information from a reputable physician, the blank school pupil applies elsewhere, and finally, as he imagines, becomes thoroughly informed.

So the young people are married. From the first they are virtually committed to a childless marriage, for they have freely given their friends to understand that it will not be convenient, for the present at least, for them to be troubled with children. They do not yet think it would be quite right to interfere with Nature when she has begun to create a human life, but they are prepared to prevent her from beginning the work. They even make a distinction in this—they will not use *active* means to this end, only *passive*.

As they are not to be troubled with the care of children, they feel free to arrange for using all their time, vitality, and means in other ways; perhaps they plan a two or three years' course of travel and study in Europe, including a course of lectures and study for the wife. All goes well for a time,* the wife remains regular, and they feel that they have, indeed, learned one of nature's great secrets. They now feel more sure of the way, and they quicken their pace; they plunge still more deeply into society and study, and extend their plans.

By and by the wife is irregular, but it is not considered anything serious; a slight chill which she got while waiting for the carriage after the opera, night before last, is supposed to be the cause of the trouble, and it is thought that all will be right by next week, if not before. But a week passes, and things are not yet right; another and another follow, a whole month, and still she is irregular. What can it mean? It certainly cannot mean conception, for they have taken the strictest precautions!

They now consult—not a physician; it isn't

* Statistics show that first children are born, on an average about 15 months after marriage of the parents.

worth while to do that—but some young married pair of their acquaintance who have had more experience than they. They find sympathy and advice, and are assured that there is no cause for alarm ; it certainly isn't conception, but simply that the cold and nervous exhaustion have combined to disturb the wife's system and interfere with Nature ; and two or three trifling remedies are suggested. A month and a week have passed, and still the irregularity remains ! The situation begins to look serious. What if it were pregnancy, after all ! There is no modification of their arrangements which would provide for a baby without great inconvenience ; and, besides, "What would people say ?"

They go again to their friends and advisers, and now learn some points which delicacy and shame had before kept back, and they finally decide to take the next step, and try if a jolting ride or a hot bath will not correct the difficulty. Nothing further than this has been suggested to them, and they still assure themselves that it is not a case of pregnancy.

But after a week or two more they are persuaded to try some "correcting pills" or other infamous nostrum which our leading dailies freely advertise under one or another thin disguise.

So they take another step. They are not yet prepared to interfere with Nature, but are quite ready merely to assist her; besides, the medicine was not bought, it was a gift from the box of the more experienced friend, who, by the way, does not mention that she first learned of it through a newspaper advertisement, which contained the following caution: "Married ladies who have any reason to believe themselves pregnant are particularly cautioned against the use of these pills, *as they will certainly cause a miscarriage*"!

There are now two courses possible. It may be that the remedy does its work; there is a period of unusually severe illness, the wife remains in bed for a week or two, and when she is again about the house finds herself languid and weak, and perhaps remains a permanent invalid, though if naturally robust and of fine constitution, she may recover her former vigor and be able to resume her usual round of work and amusement. Or the means prove inadequate to the end, and it finally becomes evident that conception has occurred and Nature intends to demand her rights.

The young couple feel annoyed and a little ashamed. The coming child is unwelcome; its parents are not in condition to give it that best of all inheritance—a good birth. During the earliest period of its pre-natal life, when the hearts and minds of its parents should be filled with loving thoughts and wise plans for the little one already dependent upon them, they are refusing to recognize it, or even seeking its destruction.

By and by it comes into the world, a feeble, fretful thing, a trial alike to its parents and to all who are about it; a kind Providence is to be thanked if such a child be not deformed or idiotic; it will almost certainly fall below a high standard of mental and moral qualities, even if it be so fortunate as to develop a symmetrical and robust physique.

After a time the pair may acquire some degree of parent-love and become rather proud of their child; but the record of wrong has been written in a human life, and may not easily be effaced; the poor child will in some way bear the evidence of having been unloved and uncared for before birth, *no after love and care being able wholly to atone for that*; and the record is, besides, written in the behavior of the parents, who, believing that society expects them to account for the remarkable fact that a child has been born to them, explain that it was an accident which they carefully guarded against, but could not prevent; or if they do not actually say this, yet in many ways, directly and indirectly, they let their friends and acquaintances know that this is the case.

It may be thought that the picture is painted in too vivid colors. Almost this very case has repeatedly come under my observation among people of standing in the world of intellect and morals.

Our young people now take active and thorough precautions against conception, and they hope and believe it will not again be necessary for them to go beyond this. They succeed for a time, perhaps several years, and then they again grow confident and careless ; or it may be that Nature demands her rights even against their vigilance, and for a second time they have family prospects. By this time they are well confirmed in their narrow, selfish life, and their one child is not such as to lead them to wish another like it. After some hesitation they decide to take the next step, and use vigorous means for regulating matters, while the life is so rudimentary and undeveloped that they are able to persuade themselves that it is a *condition* rather than a *thing*. The human mind is marvellously ingenious in the invention of excuses to a wavering conscience, and it is surprising what trifling excuses the latter is often willing to accept. In this class they need little or no instruction beyond that already received ; but in spite of their best efforts they often fail of accomplishing their purpose, and the condition continues until they are no longer able to ignore the fact that they have to do with a *thing*, and that its removal will be an *abortion*. They cast about for further instruction, and probably find it near at hand. A neighbor or a near relative has been through the experience, and assures them that it is a simple matter, advises prompt action, and offers, if need be, to assist. It seems a little like destroying a child, and they hesitate, but finally consent, but insist that an abortionist shall have nothing to do with the matter. They are very particular on this point; it would seem so vulgar and almost immoral to employ an abortionist! But the kind and experienced friend was too sanguine. Home talent runs through a course of drugs and medicines without result, and they resort to mechanical means too shocking for mention here. They are often forced to take the next step, for in their frantic efforts at removal they feel that they have effected such injury that the work must be finished at all hazards, and they call in the aid of the professional abortionist. Conscience makes a protest at each step; as they had before insisted that the work should be accomplished without employing an abortionist, so now they are very particular to have it finished *before the time of quickening*, and they feel vastly superior to those who are so depraved as to procure an "abortion" after the embryo child has shown life!

Cæsar paused on the banks of the Rubicon. So those who have had no great difficulty in their progress thus far, hesitate long before they bring their minds to cross the line and destroy a child after the period of quickening. This they only do, perhaps, when some sudden and unexpected change in their prospects and plans seems to force this course upon them after the time of quickening has come. They assure themselves that it is a painful necessity, and that they will not do it again. Their supposed necessity comes, perhaps, from business failure or embarrassment, or it may be that the wife feels ill and nervous, and seems likely to lose her beauty and her society prestige, or worse, if the gestation be not brought to a speedy close. Or it may be some matter of minor importance, such as an opportunity for foreign travel, which it is feared may never come again. No one of these would once have seemed just ground for an abortion, but by the time one has passed through the several steps already described, the mental and moral perceptions become confused, and the degrading process is rapid and easy.

We will not attempt to go into the details of the steps by which the one who has become guilty of abortion becomes an actual murderer. The pupil in this part of the course is often little more than passively connected with it, the real work being mostly done by a "coach" in the person of an unscrupulous physician or nurse, and covered under the respectable expressions "still born," or "died of infantile weakness."

In this sketch it has been assumed that the pupils were all married, and that the husband and wife were co-workers. But this is by no means always the case ; either husband or wife may do the work of almost any class, and the other, being ignorant of it and innocent of the sin against parenthood, lament their childlessness or grieve at the untimely death of child after child.

Those who look upon a doubtful action as scarcely a sin and certainly not a shame, so long as it is not found out, may think the language of this chapter unnecessarily severe. What has been described often remains concealed from the world, and so, according to their view of it, is not a shame ; but, unfortunately, there is a darker side to the picture. False modesty and dangerous ignorance in early life, indifference to children and the claims of parenthood later, and, finally, the idea that conception is easily avoided, are steps by which Satan leads on the unmarried to sin; and respectable married people are very largely accountable for this.

This is but the merest sketch of the school and its work. The details would make a volume, with chapters devoted to illegitimate children, ruined families, broken health, unloved and unloving sons and daughters, homes without wife and mother, idiots, cripples, and a very Pandora's box of social and domestic evils and crimes. There is only space for bits of shading here and there.

As before noticed, it is surprising to what an extent the laity believe that the course of Nature may safely be interfered with, even by those who understand her laws the least. Those who fear to turn back the hands of a watch lest they injure the complicated and delicate machinery, do not hesitate to use violent means to interfere with the natural working of the human mechanism, which is a thousandfold more complicated and delicate. Nature is tenacious of her rights; she resists grandly, but if forced to yield, she visits the offender with punishment which is no less sure because it is sometimes long delayed. Few seem to know this; many act as though they considered Nature a sort of clever idiot, too stupid to recognize an injury, or too amiable to resent it if discovered; while others seem to look upon Nature as rather intelligent and able, but a servant amenable to guidance and assistance in co-ordinating the forces of her laboratory. This is absurd, and even impious; for Nature is but another term for the Creator of all things, and He is infinitely wise. It may be objected that my own profession aims at assisting Nature as its regular work; in reply, I would say that no well-informed and devout physician believes that his legitimate province is anything more than to help remove the limitations and obstructions which man has, directly or indirectly, wilfully or inadvertently, opposed to Nature. It may be objected that Nature, if infinitely wise and powerful, would correct our mistakes and follies without our help. The reply is that Nature is more interested in us than in our interference with her; she cares more about correcting *us* than our mistakes and follies. Were she to go on indefinitely and patiently undoing our work, we should go on indefinitely and persistently doing it, and our wrong-doing would be righted, but we should remain in the mental or moral or physical sin which had prompted it. Indeed, if the obvious results of our sin were promptly removed, we should scarcely be aware that we were not in harmony with Nature's plans, and the race would deteriorate, and finally become extinct. But since Nature imposes on us a large share of the burden of undoing our own mistakes and follies, we are obliged to recognize them to some degree; and as it is a trouble to undo their effects, we learn to recognize them as being undesirable, even though we fail to see that they are positively sinful.

The spendthrift may have a rich father who replenishes his purse as often as it is empty, and society may appear to be no worse off because of the young man's mistakes and follies; but here is a sin against the order of things as the Creator has arranged them, and, sooner or later, all concerned must suffer for it. The father loses the blessedness of having his name maintained in honor, the son becomes a hopeless prodigal and very likely worse, and society finally must accept a member who consumes much and produces nothing in place of one who had produced much and consumed little. Had the son been obliged to earn the money to pay his debts of extravagance he would have learned the value of resources, and probably have become an honor to his father and a help to society. It is claimed by some able and honest persons that Nature herself teaches us that we are to assist her in regulating her efforts at reproduction, both in the vegetable and animal kingdoms.

I confess to a good deal of respect and reverence for the book of Genesis. Whether it be divinely inspired or not, it certainly was written by some one who knew many facts which science has but recently discovered ; and so I turn to the first chapter of Genesis for light on this point. I find it there stated that the Creator made the plants and the lower animals, and gave them into the care of man, and told him to make use of them. I also find that the Creator bade man to be fruitful and multiply, in order that he might be sufficiently numerous and powerful to do his allotted task of subduing and using Nature. Here are two distinct commands ; it is especially indicated that man is to have more or less of a struggle with Nature in the one case. In the other case, there is no command that he shall struggle against Nature ; indeed, there is no hint that man has anything more to do than to follow her leading.

Nature's efforts and apparent mistakes in the case of the woman who bears children too rapidly, and, in consequence, suffers both in her own person and in her children, and in the case of the fruit tree which bears much inferior fruit one year and none (or even dies) the next, are cited as proofs that we may properly interfere with Nature in the reproduction of our kind.

I was born and bred in the country on a stock and fruit farm, and have had a good opportunity to study some of Nature's processes, and learn some of her lessons. I have yet to see the first instance of one of the lower animals which, when left to the course of Nature, produced offspring too rapidly. I have seen plenty of instances where fruit trees bore more fruit than could come to perfection, or else bore an abundance of good fruit one year and little or none the next. This proves nothing as an argument that Nature produces unwisely, for, as we have seen, Nature had committed the fruit trees to the direction and care of man, and in many, if not all, cases it is easy to see that he alone is to blame for the fault in bearing, for he had overstimulated the productiveness of the tree, it may be, so that it had exhausted itself one year and taken a rest the next, until this had become a habit.

It may be replied that by giving attention to the matter, man may improve the quality of domestic animals, and this fact be claimed as an argument on the side of those who think that Nature needs assistance in the matter of reproduction. Nature herself arranges for the quantity of the offspring, but leaves to us much responsibility in the matter of the quality, both among the lower animals and man; and this care for the maintenance or improvement of the quality is not in conflict with the quantity which Nature, unassisted by man, produces. I have seen the quality of horses, cows, sheep, etc., improved by careful breeding, but I have never known an instance where it was necessary to interfere with the quantity in order to improve the quality. As a physician, I must admit that I have seen many children born into the world when it appeared that it would have been to the advantage of all concerned if they might not have been born; but this state of things had not been Nature's doing; it had been brought about by long and persistent disregard of her laws. She had produced no more offspring than she had provided for; but man had squandered vitality and means so that the offspring were ill-born and ill-cared for. This being noticed by intelligent people who were in the habit of jumping at conclusions while ignoring the steps which properly lead to them, gave rise to the conviction that Nature, if left to herself, reproduced unwisely, and gave us the amazing spectacle of sane and educated people preaching the doctrine that even those who were well furnished with the vitality and the means necessary to the production and rearing of a family should remain childless because Nature was producing human beings faster than she could care for them! This teaching has frequently resulted in lowering the quality of the race without reducing the number; for individuals who were well furnished for reproduction have been emboldened by it to attempt to escape the responsibility and burden of parenthood. Their attempt was a double failure; in spite of their efforts children were born to them, and under the circumstances were a far greater burden than they would have been if they had been born to willing parents.

All through the blank school there are rewards for the work done; nothing is overlooked. In the preparatory department the punishment is largely negative—*i.e.*, the pupil is kept out of a vast deal of happiness and prosperity, which only can come to those who are willing parents. This will be considered in another chapter.

Those practising "the American sin" suffer in character, because they are conscious of neglecting duty—however much they juggle with Conscience, they seldom or never entirely silence her reproaches—and they suffer in bodily health and vigor. The idea prevails that child-bearing is a pathological condition which brings in its train many discomforts and dangers.

This idea is an insult to the One who made man and instituted marriage.

If generations of foolishness and sin have brought the body to a condition of disease, child-bearing may make that condition worse, or it may possibly end the scene, just as wholesome food may distress or even destroy the person with a diseased digestive apparatus. But in a state of health, reproduction is a natural and physiological process, *and tends to the development and preservation of the individual.*

Married couples of child-bearing age ought to be ashamed to feel unwilling to become parents. There is a sense in which most of them ought to be ashamed of being unable to have children, for that means disease or incompleteness of body, and usually they or their near ancestors are to blame for it. Those who take active means to prevent conception are apt to carry the matter farther than they intended ; at the best, they are tampering with Nature, and that is a dangerous thing in itself. But in their zeal to keep regular at all hazards, they often interfere with Nature after conception has taken place, although they did not intend it. Such a miscarriage is likely to leave the system weak, perhaps invalid for life, and it is sometimes the indirect cause of death.

There are circumstances under which means

for the *temporary* avoidance of conception may be desirable and proper, as, for instance, to prevent too rapid child-bearing on the part of women who cannot nurse their infants, or who have their usual periods while nursing—conditions which, I believe, our artificial life is responsible for—and so are liable to too frequent conception.

For such and other legitimate cases Nature has herself provided a means which, with the practice of a little self-denial, will give a reasonable degree of safety ; beyond this it is neither safe nor proper to act without the advice of some physician who has sound judgment both in medicine and in morals.

Those who avoid family responsibilities are liable to intemperance in the conjugal relation ; indeed, they not unseldom avoid conception in order that they may have the greater opportunity for selfish gratification. This is one of the worst forms of intemperance, degrading alike to body, mind, and soul. When duty and pleasure are found together, they *belong* together, and may not be separated ; in just the degree that we separate them we fail of one or the other. Even taking the low and sordid ground of selfishly getting the most out of this life, it is wise to abide by temperance and duty in the marital relation, for thus, and only thus, may we derive the most possible satisfaction from it. We may drink the nectar as we will; Nature lets us hold the cup, but she mixes it herself; if we drink too deeply she adds water, then gall, and finally, it may be, deadly poison.

It is difficult to draw the line between the shades of guilt in the various classes in the blank school. The divisions which have been made are not so much those which exist in the real character of the acts as in the minds of the actors. Those in the path of sin have microscopic eyes to see the differences between themselves and others whom they consider worse. It certainly is more degrading to character to deliberately destroy unborn life than to attempt to "regulate" when there is a possibility that the life may not be originated by conception; but if married women had a proper and womanly regard for maternity, and a proper self-respect, they would not need to be told that *nothing should induce them to allow the slightest interference, directly or indirectly, with their irregularities except under the advice of an able and conscientious physician.*

Those who never intended to commit the crime of abortion upon themselves often have to bear its worst penalties, and innocently suffer in consequence of the false idea that conception is easily avoided, and that "Thou shalt not kill" was not intended to protect that which is a human life, even though it be, as yet, unborn.

The dangers of an abortion, or "miscarriage," as women prefer to call it, are very great, though they are generally supposed to be small, and, indeed, absent where the pregnancy has existed but a short time.

This is another insult to the intelligence and wisdom of Nature.

Go into the orchard where there are ripe apples and others but half grown; try to pluck one of the latter; you pull, but it does not come; you twist and wrench this way and that, and finally you secure a bruised apple with a torn and mutilated stem, and you leave behind a branch which bears unmistakable evidence of a violent and unnatural act.

Turn now to the apples that are fully ripe; you put out your hand to take one, and as you touch it, it falls gently and willingly into your open palm. If you now examine the stem and the branch from which it came, you find no marks of violence; on the contrary, both will clearly show that Nature had prepared for the separation.

Nature's course with her living fruit is much like this; in both cases the difficulty lies in separating the fruit from the stem, and in each of them this is provided for, at maturity, by a slow and sure process of degeneration of material at the point of union.

Nature is an exact and economical worker; as she is exact, she must have plans; as she is economical, she will not needlessly multiply them. So it comes about that there is but one primary arrangement for the birth of the apple and the infant.

The two great dangers in child-bearing are hemorrhage and fever; the first is caused directly, and the second often indirectly by one and the same thing—the failure of the torn blood-vessels, at the point of union between mother and child, to close properly. By the time the fruit is fully ripe Nature has so well arranged for this matter that the danger is small, but at an earlier period it is very considerable.

A vast army of women have gone to early graves, and their death certificates have read "hemorrhage," when the word ought to have been written *abortion!** Another vast army of

* I once learned of the sudden death of the wife of a pastor with whom I had been a little acquainted. Afterward meeting an intelligent and prominent citizen of the place, I inquired the particulars. The reply was substantially as follows: "Well, it was *hemorrhage*—at least it was said to have been; but it is pretty well known that it was the result of an abortion." This incident is instructive, even though the charge was unjust; for it

women who are invalids—burdens to themselves and others—ought to march under a banner bearing the same shameful and loathsome word.

In the school of Nature there are punishments for ignorance and rewards for knowledge, just as there are for vice or virtue. In these armies of the early dead and the wretched living are many who are victims of ignorance ; not a few of these are unmarried girls of good family. The facts as to this class are difficult to obtain, but are most appalling.

One of my brethren practising in a large New England city has among his patients a young unmarried woman of excellent family, whom he has attended several times within as many years, at her father's house, for what her family believe to have been simply unusually severe periods, *but which his diagnosis and her confession to him reveal as the effects of self-accomplished abortions !**

---

shows that in that community abortion was so lightly thought of that even intelligent and influential people who were friendly to the minister and his family were willing to believe that his wife died from its effects.

* Even living children are born to such without those nearest and dearest to them suspecting that they have fallen from the path of virtue ; and in the event of the early death of the infant, the matter may remain a secret. I know of such a case here in Boston.

Is it not strange that we who hold the theory that safety lies in knowledge should act on the theory, in regard to purity at least, that safety lies in ignorance? How ignorant many of our young women of good families are in respect to that which is of paramount importance to their purity and safety is little imagined! Many an innocent girl has been led on to ruin by being first made to believe that the reproductive act could not possibly be fruitful of result except at certain very limited periods, or that it must be repeated many times before there would be the conditions which would make conception possible, the argument being that as there was no danger, there could be no sin. I know a case of a boy and girl of excellent families and well brought up, in one of our large cities, who, at about twelve or fourteen years of age, had come to within a few weeks of parenthood in ignorance of the fact that for years they had habitually broken the law of God and man!

She who obtains a miscarriage in the earlier months of pregnancy feels comparatively virtuous, because she draws the line at "quickening." This is moral jugglery and ethical hair-splitting; what evidence is there of soul at five months which may not be found at four? True, the unborn child of the latter age does not appear to move its legs and arms, while the other usually does; is the spirit situated in the extremities, or is the movement of a muscle evidence of a soul? Considered from the lower plane of physical life only, what reason is there for the distinction? There has been *life* from the first; there is no *independent life* until birth. Is it reasonable to suppose that the Creator, who has been steadily at work for four months and fifteen days on one of the most delicate and complicated pieces in His whole laboratory, and has made no mistake thus far—the work being absolutely perfect as far as carried—considers it of little or no consequence to-day, but of the utmost importance and value when it shall have been in His hands a few hours longer!* Our laws visit the death penalty on the wilful destruction of post-natal human life; would that they might inflict the same penalty for the wilful destruction of pre-natal human life *of whatever age!*

In the third class we meet the abortionist. I shudder as I write the name; it is scarcely necessary to describe him, or, rather, *her*, for it is more often a female than a male—the terms man and woman would be degraded by being

---

* I am explicit on this matter, because I know that some most excellent people have wrong ideas in regard to it.

applied to the abortionist. It is a burning shame that, although we have strict laws for the punishment of abortionists, public opinion is so corrupt or indifferent that it is almost impossible to procure the conviction of one, even when tried for the second or third offence, and on evidence so conclusive as to leave no reasonable doubt of guilt.

There is dense ignorance in regard to the law about this and kindred crimes; even many physicians are not acquainted with it. I hope no one will fail to read the *Appendix* and learn what the law is. If only the popular conscience might be cultivated up to the point of approving these dead-letter laws they might be revived and used to do a needful work for our purity and protection. The State can never become the just protector of all its citizens so long as public opinion discriminates against, or is indifferent to, certain classes, be the line drawn at male or female, black or white, *born or unborn.*

The neglect of the last-named class is the more cowardly and blameworthy because the female or black person may do something for self-protection, while the unborn person* cannot; but the latter is, nevertheless, not un-

* Already virtually a citizen; see Appendix, p. 187.

avenged. Ruined health, degraded morals, decayed or extinct families, and once proud empires which live but in history are monuments to the untimely dead, and in their chronicles may be read the story of retribution for the murder of the unborn !

Difficult and delicate problems await us in the near future ; some of these seem, indeed, too difficult for us ; but the history of the past and the present should make us hesitate to declare any one of them impossible. It may seem Utopian ; nearly all ideas that are a certain distance in the van of popular consensus are considered to belong to the land of visions, yet most of the hard facts and well-proved theories of the present served an apprenticeship to Utopia in their youth ; it may be that the vision will tarry long while we wait for the reality, but I believe that just and ample laws for the protection of the rights of the family will yet be enforced, and that the State will use means to educate the citizen up to the point of intelligence in respect of all vital functions, so that ignorance shall not remain as an excuse for special sins against his descendants.

May we not look for the time when the laws shall recognize certain diseases as *crimes*, and those who induce them by their own act as *criminals ;* when a public officer, or a corps of them, shall examine the candidate for marriage to see if he or she be up to a prescribed standard for progenitors of future citizens, and when those who fall below it shall be prevented from doing the State untold injury by producing a crop of invalids, paupers, or criminals? This problem is, perhaps, the most difficult one of all. Some one has suggested that such be transported to islands of the sea, each sex by itself. There are other and more sure means, but we must advance a long way before society will have the justice and courage necessary to cope with this delicate matter. Life, liberty, and the pursuit of happiness are certainly natural rights of all, but these may be forfeited; society will yet recognize that *the citizen may lose or forfeit his right to become a progenitor.*

Our successors of a few hundred years hence will review with amazement the fact that as late as the nineteenth century the most enlightened people of the world allowed depravity and corruption to run into the streams of life, while science and philanthropy did almost nothing to purify or dry up the spring, but made the most desperate efforts to cleanse the flood!

After all, the most serious phase of the American sin is not that which concerns the children who are *not* born, but that which concerns those who *are* born under its influence; Nature is so tenacious of her rights that, be they never so unwilling, those in wedlock must now and then become parents; the children of such are born of selfishness and lust; and it were nearly as sensible to look for grapes on thorns or figs on thistles as for normal and worthy progeny from such a parentage. This point will be considered in the chapter on Heredity.*

* The postman has just brought me a circular calling my attention as a physician to the advantages offered by a Woman's Infirmary and Maternity Home located in one of our large cities. It makes a specialty of receiving "unmarried females of respectable family," who are about to be confined. The circular gives all necessary information, assures perfect secrecy, mentioning especially that the patrons are treated as "*ladies*" (the italics are in the original), and then adds: "The child will be removed immediately after birth, if we are so instructed, and the patient need not see it again. Our Articles of Incorporation give us the power to adopt it upon full surrender and the payment of twenty-five dollars. Should the mother, however, wish to reclaim it, the child can be kept for her at about twelve dollars per month, until she is prepared to do so. We are ready at all hours to send one of our physicians or nurses to any railroad depot or steamboat landing, or to any place in any State, to meet a person coming to our house; also to take charge of a child for adoption, upon receipt of the necessary expenses." It is also added that the staff are members of the County Medical Society, and that ". . . under no circumstances will a young practitioner or student be permitted to be present at a case of accouchement in one of our houses." The circular is signed by the Director, an M.D., and the Matron. I am glad to note that both have foreign names. It seems singular that this illustration came to my hand at just this time. No one of my readers can

I will not contribute to the literature of crime by explaining the details of the methods employed in the last part of the course in the blank

be so obtuse as to need that I make explanation or comment; let him carefully read these quotations two or three times, and he cannot fail to see in them a disgusting and horrible illustration of one of the easy and alluring roads by which pupils in the blank school are led on to murder, or, at least, to "adoption," the correct spelling of which is, probably, *murder!* The utmost stretch of the imagination will not cover the idea that in a land where food and service are so high that it costs twelve dollars per month to care for an infant, people can be found willing to adopt an illegitimate one and bring it up properly *for twenty-five dollars!*

It seems like the irony of fate that the protection of the State should be extended to an institution the object of which is to destroy its citizens, or if they escape with life, to make them, at the best, bastards and probable paupers and criminals. I could give many illustrations to show the source from which such an institution draws its patronage. I will give one which came to my notice within a few hours of the receipt of the circular just mentioned. A young woman of pleasing manners and fine address applied to a physician for treatment for a loathsome disease which she admitted to have contracted through sin. She gave no name and, saying that she was of good family, enjoined the greatest secrecy. Purely by accident her name and history were learned within a few days. She was the daughter of a prominent professional gentleman. She had been known to be somewhat wilful and fond of a good time—nothing more. One of these days, if she finds herself "about to be confined," she may take a freak to make a rather long visit to a neighboring city, where she can be accommodated at a "Maternity Home" and have her child—"*adopted*" for twenty-five dollars. If that course proves to be too tedious and liable to exposure, she may school. There are too many already who are adepts in the art of converting full-grown and viable babes into subjects for burial permits bearing the words "still-born," "died of infantile weakness," etc., or some other expression which covers murder under a cloak so respectable that investigation by the police seems an impertinence in a republican land.

It has been said that husband or wife might be guilty of the American sin without the other suspecting it; the work described above may be done so skilfully and secretly that even bystanders may not notice it, much less suspect that the husband or wife has been the instigator of the crime!

An extended residence in several European countries has given me an opportunity to compare their social laws and usages with our own. It does not seem that their system of espionage and repression for girls and young unmarried

---

take a short-cut to the same end by applying to a female who poses as one of New England's female doctors, but who has no medical education beyond that required to be a notorious and successful abortionist. One of her would-be patrons recently entered a neighboring house by mistake, which was only discovered after she had made her errand known and mentioned a medical man "in good and regular standing" as the one who sent her! This vile creature has repeatedly been tried for her crimes, but, thanks to her money on one side and popular indifference on the other, she has each time escaped punishment.

women would be either desirable or possible in a society constituted like ours; those who do right simply because they lack the opportunity to do wrong can never become strong and safe members of republican society. But our system of liberty and ignorance is extremely dangerous. I have to-day discussed this matter with a theological friend, who claimed that our young people could not really be in ignorance of such matters because they were continually seeing reference to them in stories. In this and in other ways, as already indicated, they certainly are learning about these things. Our street gamins are also learning about music and art from the hand organ and the theatre bill-board, but the information is even more crude and misleading in the first case than in the second one.

When the world was young and life was simple, a fortress might be built so strong that it would stand whether its defenders were many and strong or few and weak; but the world has grown mature, and society is complex and has "sought out many inventions." Now a fortress measures its strength by the men and guns which are within it. When the world was young and society simple, much ignorance and a little guarding might avail to keep boys and girls virtuous and safe; now the ignorance is impossible, and the only sure defence is that which lies in correct knowledge.

Children who are given pre-natal love and care, so that they have a clean and noble birthright, and who are afterward thoroughly and reverently instructed in regard to the nature and functions of the bodies God has given them, may be expected to possess characters which, by strength from within, will hold out against almost any attack on their virtue; when the pre-natal love and care are withheld, so that the birthright is little better than that of a child born out of wedlock, and education in these matters is left to chance—which usually means to Satan—there is usually determined a character which espionage, and even bolts and bars, may not restrain from evil, and from helping to perpetuate the worst features of the American sin.

CHAPTER IV.

THE MISSION OF THE CHILD.

"AND Jesus called a little child and set him in their midst." Such was the reply of the Master when His disciples went to Him to settle the selfish questions and angry disputes which agitated their little society. The civilized world is agitated over many sociological questions and disputes. The Divine Master has set the little child in our midst, but we come far short of comprehending the lesson we should learn from it. All problems are dark and difficult when the first step is omitted.

The little child is, broadly considered, the first factor in each sociological problem, and a factor too largely ignored the world over. So it comes about that as the one factor which is to be considered in settling the first principles of every sociological reform is neglected, those who are working, or think they are working, for the advancement of society, lack co-ordination, fail to properly understand each other and the common interests of all, and too often fall to distrusting and antagonizing those whom they should trust and help, or, worse yet, devote their energies to efforts which defeat the very ends they professedly wish to serve. A specialty is a good servant, but a bad master; a safe instrument, but a dangerous hobby. Among society's dangerous or foolish specialists we find theologians who preach as though they thought science a product of the evil one, and philanthropy a device by which love to God may be diverted to an unworthy object; scientists who refuse to recognize that which may be demonstrated by the rules of science itself, and others who profess to have a reverence for the religion of Nature, who yet are trying to learn Nature's secrets that they may thereby stab her in her secret chamber.

There are lecturers "to ladies only" who profess to be actuated simply by good-will toward their unfortunate sisters, who yet call woman's highest and holiest privilege by the name of slavery, and a law to protect the family from the first step toward extinction, tyranny.

There are apostles of woman's rights who, in their well-meaning but misdirected efforts to arouse women to claim privileges now denied them, encourage their sisters to feel ashamed of the first and highest right which is theirs by the very idea of their nature.

There are advocates of education who seek

to deter woman by false pride, from performing the one duty she is perfectly sure of being able to do better than a man! And there are those who teach that their married sisters may save time and vitality for high and noble pursuits by "electing" how few children shall be born to them, and who, indirectly, teach their unmarried sisters to take dangerous risks and commit odious crime.

Of all the well-meaning but dangerous sociologists, I believe the first place should be accorded to the disciples of Malthus, for they not only teach that the child's first and most fundamental right—the right to be born—may properly be denied it, but that it is often a duty to do this. We have already seen that the individual may forfeit his right to become a progenitor, and to prevent such an one, either by persuasion or force, is no more an interference with Nature than is the removal of a limb affected with gangrene which endangers the whole body; but to undertake the deliberate reduction of reproduction for reasons which lie outside the individual himself is quite another matter; it is a direct interference with Nature in the line of her regular and legitimate work, and, as such, it is a physiological transgression which must react upon the individual himself and upon the society of which he forms a part. It is very much like stinting the growth of the body lest there be not enough food for it when it is fully grown. In another place we will consider the question of food supply ; here we will only consider the physiological points involved in the Malthusian idea.

Interference with Nature so that she may not accomplish the production of healthy human beings is a physiological sin of the most heinous sort, for, from a physical standpoint, reproduction is the first and foremost aim and object of Nature, and she has thrown about this all the inducements and safeguards possible, even to making in man the mental and moral well-being to bear a close relation to it.

The heart of society is the home, and the heart of the home is the cradle ; without the home and the cradle it is almost impossible to make a complete and well-rounded individual, one who is well developed in body, brain, and soul, and is in ready sympathy with human life at all its stages and in all its phases. Statistics show us that Nature hedges her reproductive work so thoroughly that she shows a peculiar interest in the physical well-being of those who are at the reproductive period, and are in sympathy with Nature's purposes and plans ; this is further shown by the fact that Nature, in a measure, loses interest in the individual's physique after the reproductive work is finished, and that those who never marry do not live as long nor enjoy as good health as the married. Many believe the contrary to be true, but it is not. There are some obvious advantages which the unmarried have over the married, but these are far more than balanced by the benefits which belong to the married ; the latter are often so subtle and so interwoven with the various conditions of life that it is difficult to distinguish them, but they are there as important elements of well-being, and the insurance companies, which deal in hard facts as they find them, accord an excess of privilege to the married above the unmarried. Then, too, Nature has guarded her secrets so well that a successful interference with them is, in the long run, at a great cost, and this cost is not all charged to the guilty, but a part, at least, is placed to the account of innocent offspring.

It would be well for the world if the theologian, the scientist, the philosopher, the political economist, the philanthropist, and all the others who are working for the good of humanity, have the little child set in their midst, and learn from it that their interests are not many, but one, and that each is a coworker with all who are at work on the various problems of life, which are, after all, but one problem—in what manner and by what means to form character and bring it into harmony with the Creator and His creation. In order to this, it will be necessary for them to learn that revelation and the science of nature are but different parts of the one manifestation of the Creator. When this time comes, if it ever does, we shall have entered the millennium of love, prosperity, and peace, when each shall be a brother to his neighbor; when symmetry, strength, and beauty of mind and body shall take the place of weakness and deformity; when the Spirit of the Creator shall have an open door by which to enter the hearts of men and make them pure; when, as foretold by the seer of old, all the discordant elements of Nature shall be harmonized, so that even "the wolf and the lamb shall lie down together, *and a little child shall lead them.*" When men and women understand and appreciate the mission of the little child they will have regard for the welfare of that which may by and by be born to them, and the little-child-to-be shall lead them on to a more temperate and worthy life.

The child even before birth is able to lead the parent out of selfish thought into loving care for another. Even the "little child" which goes with its mother to another world before it has seen the light of this may leave behind it a blessing to the world in an awakened father-love which must express to other children that which it may never express to its own. Shall we ever comprehend the full power of the little child! The feeble voice may reach the ear that has been deaf to all the pleadings of duty; the little eyes may send a gleam of heaven into a gloomy life; the little hands, so weak and untrained, may yet hold two human lives together in a union of mutual love and helpfulness.

A home without a mother may be a strong and sweet and almost perfect thing, because the spirit and memory of the departed may still comfort and lead the bereaved ones and hold them together in love and sympathy; but the home which has never been hallowed by the influence of a little child can never completely fulfil the ideal of a home, and almost needs an apology for being. Those who have never known anything better may possibly feel content in it, just as those born blind or deaf are content; but they can never reach the height of maturity, usefulness, and happiness any more than can those who lack one or more of the senses.

One must be young in order to grow. God meant us to keep growing, so He has arranged that we may keep young through contact with our children. Removing ourselves from the conditions of youth and growth, we either decay or crystallize, sometimes both—the heart decays and the head crystallizes. A true marriage and a broad, complete family life ought to foster in us all goodness and make us broader, deeper, sweeter, and stronger.

Those who marry and "elect" to have no children may be compared to those about to take possession of a large, fine, well-appointed house, who, arriving at the vestibule, decide that it will be large and comfortable enough for them, and that it will be quite too much trouble and expense to occupy and care for the whole premises. Who has not seen such people in their narrow, small, and selfish vestibule life! and who has not seen divorce proceed from attempt to live together *not* "according to the ordinance of God"! And if they finally grow tired of it and attempt to occupy the whole house, they are liable to find the key lost or the lock rusty, and they may not enter; or, if they do succeed, they are likely to find the premises damaged by long neglect.

Nature never intended two individuals to live together so closely as in the relation of husband and wife without having between them children to act as buffers to properly distribute the inevitable jar and impact which will be developed in the interaction of two minds and wills in so close a relation. God never intended any love, not even that between husband and wife, to forever feed upon itself, but that it should seek and find ever wider and greener pastures. Some one, writing of the inharmonious marriage, says: "By and by comes the baby, and the baby brings love." This is often true, though if the marriage had been more harmonious the baby would have brought more love with it.

The lever is a help or a hindrance in the matter of lifting, according as we hold the long or the short end. In the work of lifting humanity the long end of the lever is the child; an enormous amount of energy and opportunity are wasted because there is so much lifting at the wrong end. It almost seems a cruel thing to say, but I believe "the highest good to the greatest number" would best be attained within the next three generations if philanthropy were to expend all its resources upon children under seven years of age; in this number I would include those who are or may be subjects for prenatal love and care.

The reformer of adults does well; he is a skilful and industrious day-laborer, whose work stops when he goes to rest. He who spends his energies upon children does better; he is an inventor constructing a machine which shall go on working after he is dead. But he who labors in behalf of children yet unborn does best of all, for he is a preformer rather than a reformer, and his work precludes the necessity for many of the laborious and painful processes of redemption and recovery. Science is striving to harness the forces of Nature for the service of poor humanity; let science teach poor humanity to use them, but also how to avoid needless poverty.

Theology is striving to regenerate individuals; let theology spend a little more of its resources in teaching how the individual may be so generated that the work of regeneration may be an easier task. Philanthropy wins its hundreds among the adults; let it win its thousands among the children, and its tens of thousands among those who are yet unborn.

The law is striving to protect ill-begotten humanity from itself; let it do something in the interests of a well-begotten humanity which will not need to be protected. Society is beginning to realize that an ounce of prevention is worth a pound of cure; let it learn that a pound of preform is worth a ton of reform. The home is an object of solicitude to those who would protect it from dangers from without; the home is in greater danger from that which is within, for the sanctity of the home and the holy relation of parenthood are used to protect crimes which strike at its very vitals. Those who look upon the child simply as the means of perpetuating the race have never learned the first lesson of life.

The mission of the child is to purify and sweeten the stream of life by bringing to it a new supply, so unsullied that it seems fresh from the spring, and purifies as it mingles with it.

CHAPTER V.

HEREDITY.

A WISE man, being asked at what period a child's education should begin, replied: "Twenty years before it is born." This was thought a strange and extravagant statement, yet it was eminently true, and struck below the mark rather than above it. The extent and importance of the law of heredity, as applied to man, are now gaining recognition, although they long have been acknowledged in regard to the lower animals. Pedigree is admitted to be almost everything in a race-horse or a pointer, and even moral qualities are supposed to be hereditary among the brutes. Many years ago I heard a stock-raiser object to using longer a certain brood mare for stock purposes, because she was mean and tricky, and her mother had been so before her; but this same man was ignorant of, or indifferent to, this principle in his own family, and the result was that he most earnestly hoped his children might not inherit traits which their mother possessed. *Ex nihilo nihil fit*, from nothing nothing comes, is a rule that is as true positively as negatively, and it works all ways and in all degrees.

Parents would be astonished and distressed if they realized to what an extent and how truthfully their children exhibited them before the world ; sins against body, mind, and soul are each punished by being reproduced in one's children, who not infrequently thus reveal that which had been forgotten, and was thought to have been forever buried years before.

As a lad I used to feel rebellious when I thought that the sins of the fathers were visited on the children unto the third and fourth generation of those who hated God ; it seemed a deliberate and cruel curse. One scarcely expects to learn Bible exegesis from anatomy, but it was through the study of anatomy that I learned the real meaning of the last part of the second commandment. One day there was brought into the dissecting-room a "subject," which was eaten, flesh and bones, by a shameful and loathsome disease such as is frequently passed down from father to son. In an instant it flashed across my mind that this was no deliberate and cruel curse, but a wise and kind lesson in regard to one of the laws of our being, and from my twenty-second year to this I have had no further difficulty with that commandment.

Parents may not excuse themselves by saying that they did nothing at all, and yet the curse appeared ; the switchman does nothing at all, and the train rushes with its living freight to swift destruction. The switchman is hanged, and just men approve. It is the privilege and duty of the parent to provide for the unborn child so that it may have a symmetrical and beautiful body, a sunny temperament, and a generous nature ; all this and much more is largely within the power of the parent, or, rather, it will be more accurate to say within the power of the *ancestors*, for everything may not be accomplished within one generation. It may happen that those who are struggling up from inherited sins and weaknesses will find themselves but partially successful in their efforts to give their children a clean record with which to begin life ; on the other hand, those who are slipping down may have one or more among their children nobler and more pure than they. Heredity is, I believe, one of the exact sciences, although we know so little of it that it seems to most persons to be almost anything but exact, and even those who have given it the most attention are often puzzled to account for its seeming vagaries.

We know some of its simpler rules, and it is

our duty to regard them carefully.* It is an established fact that the children of drunken parents will furnish a much greater percentage of inebriates than will the children of temperate ones. It is known that "love children" are peculiarly difficult to bring up in the paths of virtue.

In some families we find a fine sense of honor and a sensitive regard for truthfulness even in early years, while in others these virtues are only acquired after years of training and discipline, and always sit upon their possessors like ill-fitting garments which were bought second-hand. We know that those who are harmonious in their married life will be likely to give birth to children who are harmonious in themselves and among each other, and that strong lungs and a sound digestion may be bequeathed to one's descendants.

I know families in which there is a high average of intellectual and moral attainments, but a low average of harmony and "fitness." The

* I am rejoiced to learn that the W. C. T. U. has lately taken hold of the subject of heredity as belonging to the work of a society for the promotion of *Christian temperance.* In this they are beginning at the beginning of their task, and they will in this way be able to prevent the birth of much of the evil they have hitherto worked so nobly to reform. A pound of preform is worth a ton of reform.

members do not fit themselves nor each other, and there is continual jar and friction. There may be no lack of love and a certain sort of sympathy—they may stand ready to *die* together, but find it extremely difficult to *live* together. Looking for the cause of this state of things, we find that the parents of these families, although irreproachable in character, were unsuited to each other, and, through ignorance, it may be, had neglected to make special effort to spare their children the burden of inheriting their incompatibilities.

Even when the circumstances seem decidedly unfavorable, most surprising results may be obtained by proper regard for the laws of heredity.

The following case strikingly illustrates this.* A "love match" resulted in the union of two persons who were of nervous temperament and poor physique, many "incompatibilities," and small means. Besides this, the wife was suffering from a difficulty which made maternity undesirable and well-nigh impossible. Under the circumstances, they questioned whether an indefinite postponement of parenthood were not proper, and, in fact, clearly indicated. They considered the matter carefully, took the bene-

* The wife came under my professional care ; I give the illustration with the consent of the parties.

fit of medical advice, and finally decided that their only honorable and safe course would be that which should have a family of healthy children as its objective point. The wife was placed under medical treatment, and in the course of a few months was in physical condition safely to undertake maternity.

Recognizing their limitations and disadvantages from the outset, the young pair determined to make every reasonable effort to give the children as good a birth as might be under the circumstances. Each tried to cultivate health and strength of mind and body ; the laws of heredity were studied ; conscientious care was taken that the mother might have bright and cheery objects about her and loving thoughts in her mind during the period when each child gained all its influence from the outside world through her. Each child was also, during this period, the subject of prayer, that the Holy Spirit might enter into its developing life and cause it to be so generated that the after work of regeneration might, if possible, follow as the day follows the dawn.

It would be too much to say that this course would, in every case, be followed by results as marked as were those in this instance ; but in this family the children have proved to be, if not all that could be desired, at least much better than could have been expected in the ordinary course of events.

They are symmetrical and sound in body, equable in temperament, and affectionate toward the parents and each other. They have never been more than half the trouble and care that children ordinarily are, although possessed of high spirit and a keen sense of justice. What may develop as they arrive at maturity no one can tell, but it is certain that they now bear the impress of pre-natal love and care and a good birth. This cost the parents some effort and self-denial, but they have been repaid fourfold in the ease with which the nursery has been managed ; moreover, little differences of taste and opinion were laid on the altar of sacrifice to the interests of the children who should be born to them, and each, as it joined the family circle, brought new degrees of harmony and joy.

I have repeatedly heard the father of that family declare that he had no reason to believe himself a dollar poorer than he would have been if no child had come to claim his care. Just what might have been in that case it is impossible to tell, but it is certain that many a childless marriage which began under apparently happier auspices than this one ended in misery and divorce.

I do not believe there is any such thing as "accident of birth." That is simply a cheap and easy way of describing that which we are too ignorant or too indifferent to understand. Heredity, in its relation to the human family, is the most delicate and complicated problem that can engage the attention of the sociologist; it is no wonder that we do not yet understand all its laws; but, because we do not, we are not justified in calling its manifestations accidents. We do not yet even understand all the laws of mechanics. More than a quarter of a century ago my father bought one of Wheeler & Wilson's sewing-machines; it worked finely, but was subject to occasional fits when no amount of coaxing and oiling would avail to make it sew properly. No cause could be found, but it was discovered that usually after a short rest, sometimes of not more than a few hours, it would work perfectly. That sewing-machine still does the family sewing, but is still subject to the fits. Not being a mechanic, I have never diagnosed the difficulty; but I believe the makers have done so, and have, in a new machine, quite obviated it. These fits were almost certainly not accidental, but were the effects of some mechanical principle which was inadvertently introduced into the mechanism; it may have been so small and seemingly insignificant a matter as the unequal expansion of two metals heated by friction.

To the experienced and patient observer, the outlines of a family history may be learned from the temperaments and physiques of the children. The first born may be a morbid creature, much given to tears, and so tell the tale of the like condition of the mother during the first year of married life ; another may have a peculiarly joyous and buoyant disposition, which is the record of a quiet, happy time spent among favorable surroundings.

Still another, who is extremely prudent and economical, was born at a time when reverses in business had called for special prudence and economy from the parents ; while his more generous-hearted and free-handed brother is the chronicle of the later years when accumulated fortune enabled the father and mother to cultivate these virtues in themselves.

A time of special mental exaltation of one or both parents is often represented by a scholar in an otherwise dull family ; while the stupid child may be considered the record of a time when, for some reason, the parents had settled into the prosy routine of daily life without properly attending to the needs of their higher and better natures.

In a general way the temperaments of the

children show whether the parents began rich and grew poor, or the opposite; and whether the earlier or later years were the happier. They even expose something of the history of those parents before marriage, at times. Many a courtship which contained an episode to which neither husband nor wife will willingly refer, even to the other, is published to the world in the lustful nature and impure life of their first-born.

For nearly twenty years I have made a study of first-born children, and I am satisfied that it is one of the laws of heredity that they should resemble the father. The reason for this appears to be that in a happy marriage the husband is, during the first year, an object of peculiar interest and admiration to the wife; she thinks of him rather than of herself, and her child is patterned after the model she had before her.

The second child, under favorable circumstances, usually resembles the mother, for the reason that, having already one child like the father, both parents unite in the desire that the second one should be like the mother. When the first child resembles the mother markedly, it is occasionally difficult to account for it; but usually it will be found that the marriage was an unhappy one, or the wife was innately selfish or a chronic invalid, or for some other reason was led to think of herself rather than of her husband. Those who oppose the claims of heredity urge that children who had pre-natal hate and neglect from one or both parents sometimes prove gentle and good ; that children "of good family" sometimes cause that family sorrow and shame ; that great men are the fathers of insignificant ones, etc. All this is true, but it does not disprove the rule ; it rather confirms it.

Any one who will read the second commandment of the Mosaic Decalogue carefully will learn that the Creator distinctly affirms that He has arranged the law of heredity, and that in His accounts with His children He carries the debits through three and four generations, and the credits through indefinite generations. The debits and credits are mostly arranged according to the "fathers" of the first generation, but some of them run farther back. This accounts for much of the seeming conflict in heredity ; but there are other corrections to be made before we get the true factors of the problem. Many make the mistake of confounding reputation and character. Heredity takes no account of reputation ; it is interested in character alone. If the secret history of a family were revealed, it might be found that the son was not unlike the father in character, but in reputation. Again, repentance and tears may not wholly efface the record which sin has stamped on character, and it sometimes happens that sins of youth are passed along to children born of parents who have long walked in the ways of righteousness.

I have known many instances where sons and daughters of good family turned out badly, but I know of scarcely one where investigation would not show that the sin and evil were at some time conceived in the heart life of a near ancestor. This seems hard; but this would be an uncertain and unjust world if the vine were as likely to produce thorns as grapes, while the latter were as often found elsewhere as in the place where one would naturally look for them.

In the case of inferior children from superior parents we meet another point in the law of heredity—viz., that good care as well as good seed and good soil is necessary in order to insure a good harvest, be that harvest a crop of wheat or a brood of children. Modern agriculture laughs at the farmer who thinks to get out of the soil that which was never put into it. It is quite as ridiculous to expect to find in children that which has never been given them.

If a great man spend all his best energies in other ways, and give but the stale and tired odds and ends of interest and vitality to the important matter of reproduction, he has no right to expect that more than the stale and tired part of himself will be reproduced.

There are professional men who waste on their ambition or on their false sense of duty the vitality which is almost more than vital breath to those who are to be born to them. There are business men who, in their zeal to pile up fortunes for their children, discount the vitality of the next generation, so that it lacks either the health to enjoy the inherited wealth or the character and virtue necessary for its preservation and use. There are some saintly women who, in their zeal for foreign heathen, come dangerously near to being the mothers of heathen at home.

* * * * * *

The relation of the physician to the cemetery has been a favorite subject for humorists from time immemorial; there is a relation little dreamed of by the average maker of jokes. We learn some of our most valuable lessons from cemetery records.

In many a lot may be seen a little head-stone, which seems to say:

> "If I was so soon to be done for,
> I wonder what I was begun for?"

The date on this bit of marble may be thirty or forty years earlier than that on any other one of the head-stones.

It appears often as though what the first child "was begun for" were to prepare the way for those who were to follow; and it is early "done for" for the same reason that the sawyer casts away the first slab cut from the log. We may not accuse Nature of being wasteful nor unjust in this; she works for the highest good of the greatest number; and if we break her laws and spoil her work we may be not only content, but grateful that she deigns to repair the injury without casting away more than a part of the material damaged. Physicians see numerous illustrations of this. I will give one that came to my notice several years ago.

A courtship which had begun in a school-boy and school-girl friendship resulted in the marriage of a sound and vigorous man to a young woman who was an invalid. It was not thought that she could live more than a few years at most, but the young couple preferred to be happy together for the little time, even if it might be but a few months. They scarcely expected to become parents; nevertheless in due time a child was born to them, a nervous little sufferer, who stayed a few months and then went to rest. A physician gravely informed them that there was no hope of their having a child which could live. I was consulted about the case by a relative ; I was unable to see the persons, but from what I could learn of the circumstances, felt justified in expressing a more hopeful opinion, and gave some general advice as to manner of life, etc., in the hope that the next child might have a good share of vitality. Both husband and wife are now strong and well, and are the parents of several healthy children.

In another lot we see but two graves, husband and wife, solitary in death, as evidently they were in life.

But there is another cemetery lot with a record more sad than this one. It contains the graves ot a large family, all of whom, perhaps, lived beyond the years of infancy. The father and mother may have died at a green old age, but no one of their children lived to cross the threshold of manhood or womanhood, or, at least, died soon after doing so. More often one of the parents died in the prime of life, and some, at least, of the children lie in tiny graves. It is scarcely possible that these children could have been well born, and afterward died of injuries or from ordinary disease. No. This is a record of heredity. When one parent died young, it was probably in consequence of some disease which, passed along to the children, according to the law of heredity, caused their death, either directly or by so weakening their vitality that they were unable to withstand other diseases. The case when both parents remain strong and healthy until old age seems more difficult to understand ; but it is an open book to those who have skill and patience to read it. Heredity demands that one shall order his life so as not only to preserve himself in health, but so as to have vitality to spare for his children. The two are by no means inseparable. Those of strong constitution and indomitable will may apparently escape from suffering in their own persons for the mistakes they have made, but Nature exacts payment from their children. Such mistakes may not belong in the list of those which the law punishes—not even among those which society disapproves ; they may even be accounted high virtue by public opinion ; but Nature, taking account of character and ignoring reputation, accounts them crimes. Perhaps the guilty ones were missionaries who, with a righteous zeal which was without knowledge, undertook to convert as many heathen in ten years as would have furnished sufficient work for a lifetime ; or a minister and his wife who were ambitious to "go up higher" more rapidly than was good for their vitality ; or a merchant who, with the best of motives, made haste to be rich ; or the farmer who paid off the mortgage on his farm in five years—his wife bearing half or two thirds of the burden—when he ought to have taken ten for it.

But there is one cemetery lot which makes my heart sick—it is the one with a long row of infant graves. The devout lay observer is wont to exclaim : " What a mysterious Providence !" It certainly is both mysterious and providential—mysterious how the parents could have been guilty of bringing those infants into the world, and providential that the morbid, weakly things were removed soon, and not allowed to cumber the earth, a weariness to themselves and others. And there is another mystery about it—that the parents were willing thus to advertise their weakness and their sin. It had been better to have let the kindly hand of time level the dishonoring little mounds of earth, and to have put the chronicle, if anywhere, on the least conspicuous place on the family monument. One, two, even three infant graves may call for sympathy for the bereaved parents ; but when the number reaches a half dozen or more, sympathy often may well be swallowed up in pity and its near of kin, contempt ! Behind this row of tiny graves there usually lies a loathsome disease, which might have remained a secret had not heredity published it to the world.

There is another disease which is born of sin, and which leads to grave results, although it is popularly believed to be a small matter, easily and quickly cured, and leaving no trace behind it. This disease sometimes lies behind the cemetery lot with only the graves of husband and wife. Children had been desired, and it had been thought a mysterious Providence which withheld them. Investigation might have explained the matter in this way. The husband contracted this disease; he was apparently quickly cured, and supposed that to be the end of it; but the end was not yet. He gave the disease to his pure and innocent wife, in whom, perhaps, it was never recognized at all; but it did its work—the inflammation which it caused thickened the walls of delicate tubes in the mechanism of reproduction; they were stopped up, and she became barren.

Heredity is a solemn fact, and an inexorable factor in human weal and progress. It is an unwelcome truth to very many because it "tries the reins and searches the heart" of individual life as nothing else can do. It is, in its way, a sort of religion, too, and it is a preacher of righteousness; for the individual must hold himself back from *all* intemperance in the use of mental and physical faculties, and keep himself in harmony with Nature's laws, if he would not have his sin find him out, and appear in mental, moral, or physical unloveliness or deformity in his descendants.

The Divine Master said: "Do men gather grapes of thorns or figs of thistles?" Yet humanity was at that time trying to do this very thing, and humanity is trying to do it still.

In undoing a tangle of thread there is always a temptation to work at the loops; by pulling these they may be made larger, and apparent progress result; but the beginning and the end of the loop are still lost in the mass, and too often this has been made tighter than it was before. The only sure way is the slow and tedious one, which patiently finds one of the ends and works from there. Heredity teaches the reformer an important lesson; he too often looks for grapes from thorns, or spends his energies in the effort to fit the thorns to some useful purpose when he might as well be cultivating grapes. He rescues a few individuals, but the great stream of human life meanwhile rushes by him on its way from sin to destruction.

A pound of preformation is worth a ton of reformation. The reformer, striving to cure, has the odds against him, and must meet with virtual defeat. The preformer, striving to prevent, has an apparently slower and less promising task, but the end, though it may be far off, must be glorious success. The sociologist who begins at the beginning of his work must lay the foundation for safe and desirable heredity for those whose parents are yet in childhood, and an indispensable part of his work will be to teach the responsibility and blessedness of parenthood.

In this chapter we have considered the dark side of the picture more than the bright one; but the picture is not all dark. He who visits the iniquities of the fathers upon the children unto the third and fourth generation also shows mercy unto thousands of those who love Him and keep His commandments. And He has also said: "The promise is unto you *and your children.*"

CHAPTER VI.

WOMAN'S WORK.

NATURE clearly indicates that woman was intended to be man's companion and coworker. Nature arranged that woman should be man's equal—not that she should be his equivalent nor that she should do a man's work—that she should bear her fair share of the burdens incident to life, and should have her full share of the compensation. In her arrangements, Nature trusts her children with certain details, and if her children prove inefficient or untrustworthy, she is often made to bear the blame. Her arrangement of a division of labor between man and woman is wise and just; but men and women have been unwise in carrying out the details of her plan, and injustice to both, especially to woman, has resulted.

Broadly considered, Nature arranged that man should be the provider of means of subsistence, and that woman should be the dispenser of these means.

In this arrangement woman is at somewhat

of a disadvantage with man, because he stands nearer the source of supply, and if he choses to disturb the balance of affairs, he finds it easier, for a time, at least, to selfishly keep all for himself and do his own dispensing than woman does to win her own supply. The balance of affairs between men and women has become much disturbed ; man is prone to make woman his plaything or his slave, or to neglect her altogether ; and woman, crowded out of the place God meant her to fill, and finding much difficulty in regaining that place, is in many instances making another place for herself by becoming a bread-winner.

This is proper and, indeed, necessary on the part of many, and it will tend to readjust society on a natural and healthy basis, provided woman keeps clearly in mind what her natural and permanent position is, and does not forget that as a bread-winner she is in an unnatural or temporary one. Unfortunately, many women have forgotten this, or have inherited forgetfulness of it from their mothers, and so we have the sad spectacle of women who advocate female independence as an end and not a means—as an end, making her man's equivalent ; and not as a means, bringing her back, by and by, to her proper position as man's companion and co-worker—his complement.

We believe the Creator to be omnipotent, therefore He might have made each individual of the human species complete, fully furnished to sustain and reproduce; but He has not so made man, but has wisely, as we believe, given man a division of labor.

In considerations of this question, I believe a grave mistake is made in that man's work is considered first. Woman listens in respectful silence to the end, and then exclaims: "Well, as far as regards the industries, there is no reason why *I* cannot do all that." And it is perfectly true. A wise Creator has arranged it so in order to provide for the possible contingency of man's forcing woman to take care of herself.

But without going into the details of man's work and his superiority over woman in it, let us consider woman's work. In the first place, it certainly *is* woman's work, for it cannot be done by a man, however willing a man might be to do it; and, in the second place, it is absolutely necessary, for the world would soon come to an end without it; in the third place, it is a more honorable and important work than man's; and, finally, if woman does her work well and thoroughly, it requires all her time and vitality. So woman is debarred from doing a man's work not because she *cannot* do it, but because her own work is all she can possibly attend to.

The key to the question, What is woman's work? is the fact that Nature has imposed on her the most of the burden of reproduction. The rest of woman's work follows naturally, for as she is brought into peculiarly close relations with the human individual at its tenderest age, when it requires to be treated with the greatest gentleness and tenderness, and to have the smallest details of its daily and hourly recurring wants thought of and cared for by another, the Creator has endowed woman with a special store of the gentler and finer qualities of mind and heart, and has given her a peculiar adaptability for planning and executing little details connected with the distribution of means of subsistence to the ends of the comfort and happiness of those about her. But in doing this, woman is the home-maker and housekeeper, and this is just what God meant her to be—just this and nothing more. Perhaps some woman who has read these words will exclaim: "Yes, he is like all the rest; he believes that woman should be confined to the narrow round and petty details of domestic drudgery!" There is the cant of sociology as well as the cant of religion. I believe the words "narrow round," "petty details," and "domestic drudgery" to be among the most offensive cant expressions that belong to the social problem, and they only belong to woman's work when it has been so belittled and degraded from what God meant it to be that it is scarcely recognizable. Woman's work is what she makes it, and she may make it less narrow, less petty, and less like drudgery than man's work is, if she will. An able writer on this subject has said that in the division of labor woman is at a great disadvantage with man because she must do the one thing, housekeeping, while man may take his choice from all besides this—virtually that a man may choose his calling, but woman can have but one in any case. The exact opposite of this is far nearer the truth. A man is a bread-winner, and this task usually confines him to a narrow round of duties which he performs day after day, often with so little variety that he feels almost like an automaton; often it is worse than this, for in the fine and exact divisions of labor in the large manufacturing industries, a man is frequently little more than a small part of a machine, and his success depends upon his working as much like a machine as possible. Whatever the social or intellectual grade of the man, he is the bread-winner, and his wife is the bread-dispenser. The latter work is a higher and more honorable task than the former one. Incidentally man may have contact with various interests in his work, and may serve human weal in many ways; but, nevertheless, the object of his work is to win bread, and this object is, as a rule, constantly in his mind. Woman's work, on the contrary, is as a distributor, and this gives her interests as broad as all human needs and brings her into the closest personal relations with others. Man's work is impersonal, woman's personal; persons are always more interesting than things, and so a woman's work is more interesting than a man's. It may be objected that a man also comes in contact with persons in his daily round of industry. He does and he doesn't; he certainly meets others in his daily round of work, but, as a rule, he meets them in a selfish way—that is, he is bread-winning; his bread-winning requires that he should meet others, and he meets them mainly for the sake of what he can, directly or indirectly, get out of them. Such contact as this can scarcely be said to be contact at all. It certainly is not the contact which best draws one out of self and lifts him above the sordid things of earth and sense. It may be said that this is a low and unworthy view of man's work as a bread-winner; that may be, but it is a fair statement of what bread-winning actually is among the majority of those in the trades and in business, and too frequently in the learned professions.

Woman's work, on the contrary, requires her to come into the closest contact with others, less for her own advantage than for theirs. She is the real maker of the home and the queen of the household; husband and children look to her to take dollars which of themselves are as unmeaning as bits of clay or stone, and convert them into light and warmth and music and art and books and food and drink and clothing and all else which go to make up the visible and palpable factors of a home; but woman's work is better than this, for husband and children look to her to fill the place with love and sympathy and tact and a ready interest in each and every one of them, and to infuse an air of gentleness and grace over all, without which no quantity or quality of material things could make a *home*.

But best and noblest of all the work that belongs to woman is maternity. In this she is also a distributor, for she may use all the material resources that come to her hand in such a way that they shall conduce to grace of mind and heart and person in herself, and through her be distributed, indirectly at least, to the members of the next generation. It may be said that woman does not do this work alone;

that she receives help from man. To some degree this is true, but man's part in the distribution of character to the next generation is a subordinate one. Any one who doubts this needs only to study the history of families with good mothers and bad fathers, and those with bad mothers and good fathers. There are countless examples of good mothers who have brought up large families of children who turned out well, although they had little for which to thank their fathers. We sometimes see the reverse experiment tried; I have never known an instance where it was a success. It is true that the wife with a bad husband may not expect to accomplish as much with her family as she might do if she had the help which her husband should give her, and if he be markedly bad she runs great risk of having one or more of her children inherit more or less of his badness; but under these adverse conditions she may yet make her family a virtual success if she will; while the father, working under the like conditions, usually finds his family a virtual failure. It is not an easy matter to account for this. We see numerous examples of children inheriting one and another quality and tendency from the father, and in a given number of examples these may seem to cover all the essential points of character, and yet the father who is not properly supported by the mother is a failure as a progenitor. The mother appears to transmit the co-ordinating moral forces without which it is impossible to make a strong and successful human life.

Some may claim that, granting all this, the woman's position is a narrow and monotonous one as compared with the man's. Let us look at a few examples.

The wife of the day laborer living in three rooms, and having all the work to do for her husband and several small children besides herself, usually has a busy life, and a hard and monotonous one as compared with many more fortunate people. She bakes and washes, makes and mends, sets tables and washes dishes, dresses children and undresses them again in a round which ends only with the day, and must be taken up again on the next; yet her life is not without variety—in fact, each day is full of it; from the time when she arose at five in the morning to make the fire for her husband's breakfast, or to nurse the baby, until she lays down her darning at bedtime, she has given her attention to processes which, if organized into money-making industries, would make a half dozen trades, besides doing a number of other interesting things. What has her husband been doing meanwhile? He went to his work, dinner-pail in hand, at early morning, joined the horse, cart, and two or three fellow-laborers with whom he has worked until not one of the company possesses a new idea or story with which to entertain the rest, and—shovels sand until twelve o'clock. He then sits under the shadow of the cart and eats his cold dinner and takes a nap or smokes until one o'clock, when he again shovels sand until six. Which has had the narrow, monotonous round of work! But it may be claimed that the man's labor ends at six, while the woman must work until nine or ten, and the objector quotes the couplet which has so often done service before:

> "Man's work extends from sun to sun,
> But a woman's work is never done."

This is sometimes true, but so is it that

> "Man's work extends from sun to sun,"
> While a woman's work is not begun.

In the case of the laborer and his wife we not infrequently see that the wife rests during the evening, while her husband, who has worked hard for ten hours already, works the whole evening long at rude carpentry or something else which will increase the convenience or comfort of their simple home. The husband rested for an hour at noon, but the wife has very likely rested more than this; and even when most hurried with her work, she will usually find a little time to read, if she likes, while nursing the baby. In the matter of companionship she has had the advantage of her husband, for besides the occasional "running in" of this or that neighbor, whose varied interests always furnish some interesting topic of conversation, she has her children, and a child, with its developing powers of mind and body, furnishes variety and entertainment for any one who is near it, and may almost furnish a liberal education to any one who studies it intelligently and carefully.

Going higher, we find that the skilled mechanic or the small tradesman has more variety and entertainment in his work than the day laborer has, but his wife still has the advantage, for besides having the wide range of duties which the laborer's wife found in her life, she is in very many cases able to keep a servant, and have a good share of time and vitality for the cultivation of her mind in various ways, and for amusement.

If we look at the mercantile and professional classes, we find the advantage vastly on the side of the wife, for her husband not infrequently works like a slave during fourteen or more hours of the twenty-four; but this work is often of the narrowest and most monotonous sort, like adding columns of figures, or watching the fluctuations of stock quotations, or attending a round of patients with symptoms which for years have been as familiar and uninteresting as the homeliest household words. And this round of duties often, usually, in fact, requires so much time and vitality that the man has little of either to spend in amusement or in broadening his education, so that one of the common occurrences is for an intelligent and successful merchant or professional man to be so narrow in his education and cultivation that he can talk of little else than shop. Compare this with his educated and cultivated wife, who need do little or no domestic work that money will hire some one else to do for her, who has ample time and vitality for the cultivation of literature, art, and music, and may acquire breadth of information through much travel at home and abroad. There are thousands upon thousands of such cases in America where the wife's position is immeasurably superior to her husband's, with the single exception that he stands nearer the sources of supply than she does.

It is said—and has been said so many times that most people seem to believe it—that man's industrial position insures him a better and broader education than his wife or sister enjoys.

I do not know how it may be in all parts of the country, but *in New England the average wife is better educated and is broader in her intellect and culture than her husband—is, in fact,* "*too good for him.*"

But, whatever the dignity of woman's special work, many women are denied the privilege of enjoying it, because some of those who are married are treated as playthings or slaves, and others have no opportunity to marry at all, because many men prefer to remain single. I believe a woman obliged to work for her daily bread is a blot on creation, as the Creator intended it to be ; yet I feel sympathy with much of the so-called Woman's Rights Movement, because I question whether it will be possible for woman to acquire and hold her natural and inalienable right to be supported in dignity as wife and mother until she has " carried the war into Africa" and acquired the unnatural and alienable right to take care of herself. When she has done this she may, perhaps, use her independence to dictate and secure reasonable terms in her relations with the other sex.

I feel sympathy with nearly every effort that has been put forth by earnest and true women for the advancement of their sisters. I must say, however—and I say it with great reluctance—that I believe many of those who have been connected with the Woman's Rights Movement, and, at least, some of the advocates of higher education for women, have been to blame for disseminating opinions and theories which, indirectly at least, have aided and abetted the sin against maternity. In many cases, certainly, nothing of the sort was intended. Their words, as construed by the pure and intelligent woman, may have had no bad influence; but not every woman who has read or heard these words has been very pure nor very intelligent. And so there has grown to be a feeling among many women—some of them good and true ones, too—that the duties of maternity are a sort of low-grade drudgery which properly may be left to those who lack the will and the ability necessary to carry them into a higher sphere. Education, influence, leadership are all desirable, and a woman has a right to desire them; but if she acquire them at the price of her privilege of wifehood or motherhood, she has paid too dearly for them, and can never use them in a cause so high and noble that it will atone for the sin of selling her birthright. Some of our noblest women, who are proud of being the mothers of families, feel in their hearts a tendency to grudge the time and vitality demanded by the nursery.

I once knew a woman who was prominently

connected with a popular and important reform movement; I had supposed her childless, but met her one day leading two beautiful children. Learning that they were her own, I congratulated her on her good fortune, when she drew a weary sigh and replied, "Yes, but they are an awful sight of care."

When heredity is better understood it will be recognized that, in the long run, nations are made or unmade according to the love and care bestowed upon children before their birth, and the influence they receive in the nursery; then, and not before, will woman learn the dignity and blessedness of maternity, and she will redouble her endeavors to acquire and use her every right and to drink more deeply at the fountain of knowledge—not that she may fill a sphere higher than maternity, but prepare herself to fill that sphere so well that her descendants may be of earth's noblest and best. It has been said that a woman may bring up a family in respectability even when that family inherits little or no good from the father; this is true even when the mother is weak, provided some woman of strength of character comes to her rescue. Some years ago I learned of a case which strikingly illustrates this.

A somewhat strong-minded woman, who had no false ideas as to woman's sphere, and who had brought up a large family of her own, besides "lending a hand" to a number of her less fortunate neighbors and friends, found herself at the age of sixty with a little spare time and vitality, and decided to undertake the reformation of a family belonging to the pauper and criminal classes. She chose a family living in the greatest degradation. The father was a jail-bird, the mother not more than half bright. In point of intelligence the children ranged from a total idiot to one who was decidedly promising.

The mother had given her children pre-natal love and care so far as she could, and crowned the after love she gave them by committing the youngest two to the entire care of her benefactress, although that meant their entire separation from her, and she loved them devotedly.

That family was lifted out of the pauper and criminal class; several of the children became church-members, and the two who were removed from the rest of the family became representative people of the town in which they lived.

This incident never became known outside the locality where it occurred. This reformer never became a popular heroine, never received the applause of admiring audiences, nor saw her name in print. She worked quietly, often without the sympathy of those nearest and dearest to her, sometimes without the gratitude of those whom she served; yet she labored patiently on, never halting, never doubting, always giving her own personality to her chosen task.

There are hundreds and thousands of noble American women who are doing this sort of work. They are our really strong-minded women, for it requires more character, conscience, and will to do this than to carry on an arm's-length contest with abstract evil when the better part of society forms an admiring audience.

I rejoice in the recent advance in the higher education of women. I believe it rests on solid ground and has legitimate ends, although some of its advocates have somewhat mistaken its real meaning, and have claimed too much for it.

It is interesting to study the history of the movement and see how its enemies have continually retreated before its advance. At first —long ago, fortunately—it was claimed that it was wicked to educate a woman. But inspiration uttered no certain sound on this matter, and by and by light came, and the civilized world "moved on" from that barbarous idea. Next, it was claimed that she was incapable of education. Science investigated the subject and found that the woman's brain was exactly like the man's except that the latter was larger in proportion to his greater weight and bulk. While science was puzzling over the strange phenomenon of an animal with an organ for which it had no adequate use, women explained the mystery by taking college prizes away from their less able or industrious brothers. Society was surprised, but finally decided to laugh and retreat behind the claim that, although woman has the intellect, she lacks the physique necessary to the attainment of a higher education. Some good fighters—and able physicians are among them—still remain at this point. I believe science has refused to furnish aid or comfort to either party, but Wellesley, Smith, Vassar, Mt. Holyoke, and other like institutions seem to be winning frequent victories for the women. The most advanced enemies of the higher education of women are those who admit that she can acquire a scientific education, but deny that she can satisfactorily use it when she gets it. Educated women doing effective work in professions in this and other countries have answered this objection again and again.

It seems to me that two mistakes are often, if not usually, made by the more enthusiastic advocates of the higher education of women: one is that it should be acquired between the same years that a man's higher education is; the other, that its object should be to make woman, in as far as possible, man's equivalent. These are two grave mistakes. I believe there is neither mental nor physical bar to a woman's getting as thorough an education as her brother; but I do believe that Nature protests against her attempting to get it at as early an age. The reason for this is not far to seek. Embryology teaches us that the female is a higher order of being than a male of the same species. The rule is, the higher the order, the slower the development. This is true in man. The male is developed at an earlier age than the female, and is, besides, so much less complicated and delicate that he can bear much greater mental and physical strain during the years of development than the female can. It is foolishness, therefore, for women to attempt to acquire a higher education at as early an age as their brothers do. They *can* do it, but not with safety; they usually discount health and strength for themselves or for their children by doing it. Dr. Emmet believes a woman should not attempt to finish a higher education before she is twenty-five years old. That is certainly none too old. (See Note on page 151.)

The object of a woman's education should be to fit her to be a man's coworker and complement—*not* his equivalent—though in the present ill-balanced state of things she sometimes seems forced to be man's equivalent as nearly as may be. The question now seems to be, Ought women to enter the various industries and professions or not? There seems no question that some must do so in the present state of society, but the great majority ought not.

Nature produces a few more women than men.* Could she justly deny them the means of self-support? In various ways society increases the disparity by destroying men in war, etc., and by unequally massing those who remain; and society is in duty bound to provide some compensation for this disadvantage. Finally, there is a class of men who might marry, but will not; consequently there is a class of women who should marry, but cannot. Those who are to blame for this abnormal state of things ought to be held accountable for it. May the time come when the State will settle accounts between the parties by taxing single men and devoting the proceeds to the industrial education of single women who are able to work, and to the support of those who are not; and may the tax be so heavy as to make it an inducement to escape it through marriage.

* This is doubted by some. It is true in the civilized lands.

It is not so very many years since the authorities of great cities decided that to attempt to stay the plague by cleaning the streets would be an impious act, showing a lack of confidence in Providence! Now the people who should neglect to do so would be thought to tempt Providence, and would be compelled by public opinion to do it as belonging to the common safety. The sentiment of society now is practically this, that people may marry or not as suits their personal convenience; and if they marry, may marry whom they please outside the line of near kinship. We shut our eyes to the plain teaching of Nature, and make for ourselves rules and regulations which are absurd and even puerile. Could we have a more marked example of this than that a people as civilized as the English allow mental, moral, and physical deformity to go on reproducing itself *ad libitum*, while it forbids a man to marry his second cousin or his deceased wife's sister! If every Englishman who has married within the last hundred years had married his second cousin, and every one who became a widower had straightway married his sister-in-law, the mental, moral, and physical disturbance of society would not have been a tithe of that which has been caused by the descendants of "Mother Jukes"!

Marriage is so intimately connected with the weal of society that I believe the time will come when the State will recognize its duty to provide, not only that the unfit shall not marry, but that the fit shall marry.

A vast stream of corruption is constantly being poured into society because those who were in condition to marry and lead honorable and useful lives preferred to lead selfishly single and corrupt lives.

Men complain that they cannot afford to marry, and they berate society for this state of things. Man's love of luxury and his silly pride are oftener to blame for this than are the same qualities in women. If women must work, it is but fair that they should have honorable and remunerative employment, and every honorable man ought to feel some measure of personal responsibility for this; but any honorable man who is able to support a wife and family, and is not doing it, ought to consider carefully whether he is not living below the line of privilege and duty. Man's first duty to woman is to provide that she shall not be obliged to support herself. A man's duty to any woman who is obliged to support herself is to do his best to assist her to this end. Paid female labor has a near and a remote object, and the latter one is the more important. The immediate object is that the individual female shall have means of subsistence; the remote object is to restore the balance of society by refusing man the privilege of using woman as a toy or a slave.

If a man has wronged a woman, either by stealing from her outright, or by refusing her work, or by under-paying her, or by neglecting to marry and support her in dignity as wife and mother, he has no right to complain if she force her way into serious competition with him in the higher industries and professions.

I, for one, say, live and let live, or, better than that, live and help live, to the 70,000 supernumerary women of Massachusetts, and to the thousands of others who are in the industrial ranks because no man hath married them.*

Those who claim that woman ought to support herself say that many—possibly more than

* There are women who are single from choice. I believe there are many who are unmarried because they never met those who sufficiently aroused their interest and respect to lead them to look upon them as possible husbands; many of the latter, I dare say, have even never had an offer of marriage, simply because their self-respect and sense of honor prevented them from allowing a declaration of love which they felt they could not return. Many a woman who has never had an actual offer of marriage has, nevertheless, had ample opportunity to marry if she had cared to do so. But this and other phases of the woman question which do not involve first principles cannot be enlarged upon in these few pages.

half—of the families in the world could not make both ends meet but for the income-producing labor of the wife and mother, and they make the further claim that a higher order of vitality is found among the hard-worked peasant women of Europe than among the well-to-do women of America. As to the first statement, it may be said that the state of society which requires woman to be a wage-earner is an abnormal and corrupt one. All the female wage-earners in the world will not earn enough to pay to-day's bill for extravagance and vice. The second claim is not sustained by the facts—the opposite is true. Of a given number of female infants who are born under the two conditions, the greater per cent will be found alive and in health at eighteen years of age among the well-to-do class in America, and at fifty years of age the advantage is vastly against the laboring woman. No one can doubt this who has mixed with the daily life of the peasant class of Europe and seen how their women get past their prime at thirty and are old and feeble at fifty—the age when many an American woman, who has not exhausted her vitality by luxury and frivolity, is in her prime, and at the acme of womanly attractiveness.

Many men seem to fear that if women once become self-supporting they will be unwilling to marry and rear families; were this true it would but be a case of showing men that "what is sauce for the goose is sauce for the gander." In this busy, mercenary age we have learned to place too high a value upon that which money will buy and too little respect upon that which money cannot purchase; and it is true that too many capable girls have the idea that, in order to show their smartness and capability, they must show themselves smart at making money and capable of taking care of themselves; but it is also true that Nature seems to have a stronger lien on woman than on man; for although many men who might marry will not, the average woman who has earned an honorable and lucrative position for herself seems to be very willing to marry when a suitable opportunity offers.

A woman should have the highest and best education which circumstances allow, because, other things being equal, she is a better wife and mother if well educated.

Many claim that a higher education hardens a woman and partially unfits her for domestic life. I believe this is not true, unless the education has been crowded into early years, which belong to the special development of her womanly functions and balance.

I have had fair opportunity to study the *per-*

sonelle of a celebrated female college of which Massachusetts feels justly proud, and I fail to see any seriously hardening or unsexing influence from it. On the contrary, it has always seemed that both faculty and students showed a high degree of strictly womanly qualities; even that those in the highest positions and the best scholars appeared fitted, both by temperament and culture, to shine in domestic life. I make the acknowledgment with the greater pleasure because the discovery was an agreeable surprise.

Is the estimation in which fashionable society holds babies fairly illustrated by the rule which sends them out on the street in the care of a servant, while it is the correct thing for the mother to appear with a pet dog in her arms?

I am surprised that so many otherwise sensible and wise mothers have allowed themselves to follow this wicked and contemptible custom. It is cheering to note that many women of position are asserting their womanhood and courage by substituting the baby for the dog.

When we become thoroughly civilized we shall hear very little about woman's rights, because then woman will be in the full enjoyment of the one right which embraces all others; we shall seldom hear woman talk about a career, and she will then express regret that a career is necessary for her. There will then be much less talk about higher education of women, because that will be a matter of course for those who need and wish it. There will be little complaint about women in the industrial ranks, because the few who will be there will have good and sufficient reason for it.

But we are not fully civilized yet; generations may pass away before we shall be. In the mean time, woman must fit herself to survive in the unnatural position into which she is forced, and preformers must seek to produce men and women who will be willing to undertake the duties and compensations of life as God intended them to do. When that time comes, men will not hesitate between paternity and selfish ease, women will not hesitate between maternity and a "career," nor will a pug dog be a more respectable care than a baby.

Note to page 143.

In order to the safety and comfort of the young woman student, four things should be borne in mind: 1st. Digestion is less a matter of what one eats than when and how he eats it; it is absurd to expect good digestion with a tired stomach and a busy brain; a few minutes' rest before dinner, and a half hour's rest with a five-minute nap afterward would cure many a dyspeptic and restore many a tired brain to working condition. 2d. Regularity of the bowels should be expected and demanded; it is a physiological *crime* to allow them to be habitually torpid, as many young women students do. I would even make it a misdemeanor for a student to fail to report to the matron a single day's irregularity. 3d. *Vitality* as well as *time* should be allowed for recreation; change of work is *not* in itself rest. 4th. And last, but by no means least, one or two entire days out of each twenty-eight ought to be given up to physical and mental rest; this should not simply be *allowed*, it should be *required*, and the curriculum ought to allow for "making up" the studies without borrowing time or vitality from recreation.

CHAPTER VII.

OVER-POPULATION.

It would be unfair to assume that all who seek to avoid the parental relation are actuated by vicious or unworthy motives; people of decided cultivation of head and heart are found among these, and some of the reasons which seem to them good and sufficient for their course are over-population, ill-health, poverty, and the discomforts and dangers of child-bearing.

The danger of over-population being considered a serious matter by some intelligent and sensible people, others, who are neither intelligent nor sensible, are encouraged to use means, be they fair or foul, to avert the calamity.

Some portions of Europe and Asia are uncomfortably crowded, but it is probable that they might support a much greater population than that which they now have if society were arranged on a proper basis.

North and South America, Australia, Africa, and many islands of the sea contain but a fraction of the inhabitants they might well support, even with the present industrial knowledge and appliances. Add to these new discoveries in science and natural resources, with a steady growth in providence and virtue, and the imagination may scarcely set a limit to the number of people who might live on this earth in comfort and prosperity. It is difficult to say just what, in kind and degree, the progress of the next few hundred years may be, but we have hints of the future from the past and the present. When electricity is more fully known and applied to daily use; when the sun's rays are caught and harnessed for our use to give us light, heat, and mechanical service by day and night, and when we learn to use, and not waste, the larger part of what the lavish hand of Nature pours into our laps—when this comes—and I do not doubt that it will come before this world is seriously over-populated—it will doubt less bring with it numbers and vastness of resources not now dreamed of by the most sanguine.

Too many of those who have given attention to the relations between population and food supply have made the mistake of assuming that the one increased by geometrical progression and the other by arithmetical progression. This, were it true, would give us cause for the gravest anxiety for the near future. According to this theory, the world is steadily growing bankrupt ; but the theory is not true, fortunately, and this old world is steadily growing richer in the ability to feed and clothe the members of the human family. A deal of misunderstanding arises from confounding the words consumption and destruction. Consumption, as applied to food, does not mean destruction ; nothing is or can be destroyed ; we can change its form for a time—that is all. We burn a tree, but when we have finished the operation Nature is in possession of the water, gas, and ash which composed it, and can go to work and make another tree or other form of vegetable life with them, and, in fact, she does do it if we but give her time. We only borrow the food which we eat and incorporate into our physical systems. Nature is the lender ; she holds good security for the loan, and will certainly call it in sooner or later and devote it to the use of some other one of her children. More than this, Nature secures good interest on her loans to us, for, broadly considered, her resources are increased in value by our use of them. Brains are a large factor in the food problem.

Physical Nature is not a storehouse of resources for the production and preservation of life ; *it is a machine*, and the quantity and quality of the product depend largely upon the brains brought to bear upon the running of it.

Probably this machine will not run forever, but we have every reason for believing that it will last for many millions of years yet.

There is certainly a good supply of solar light and heat, and there is no scarcity of water. There is a limit to soil capable of supporting vegetable, and so, animal, life, but the laws and forces which created what we now have are still at work making more, and we do not destroy any of it. Sometimes we fail to put things back where they belong, and limited sections grow barren; but the fertility, or that which makes it, is all safe somewhere, and sooner or later Nature will work it up again for our use. Although this earth is not a storehouse of food, but a machine for producing it, yet Nature does, as a matter of fact, furnish us some store of food in the form of fish and game and the plant life which flourishes without our care; but all this store is a mere trifle, a sample, as it were, which Nature turns out to show us how the machine works. It is estimated that human brain and muscle can produce more than fifteen hundred times as much from an acre of land as Nature usually gets out of it alone. Human effort attains results nearly if not quite as brilliant in fish culture and in other directions. The food supply and the ease and comfort of life have steadily increased with the increase of population, and there is to-day more and better food per capita of the human family than there was hundreds of years ago, and the increase has been almost without break.

There is a limited quantity of plant-sustaining soil, but even this is not a fixed quantity. This earth is not yet completed. Nature is still at work on it. We are fully aware of this when an earthquake shakes us about or even engulfs the results of our labor. Few realize, however, that our earth is having solid matter added to it all the time. This is from the waste material of other worlds, and comes to us in the form of cosmic dust; it is estimated that this amounts to five hundred thousand tons in a single year. So Nature is shifting about the illy-balanced portions of the earth; she is still adding to its quantity; she is still at work making productive soil out of unproductive rock, and is still increasing the fertility of that soil by taking valuable material from the sun and air and putting them into plants and animals, and through them into the earth; and, finally, man is rapidly learning how to get more and better results from Nature's resources. Will any one dare affirm that food increase can only be at the rate of arithmetical ratio?

Just a few words about the geometrical ratio of human increase: it is theoretically true, but not actually, and it is so far from true that, as already noticed, man stands in a more favorable relation to food than he did hundreds of years ago. One of Nature's laws is that there shall be a certain amount of compensation allowed to any form of life for the disadvantages with which it is burdened. Accordingly, the lowest forms of life, those which have least ability to protect themselves, are enormously prolific, and those better provided with means of locomotion or defence are less so. This rule holds through the lower animals, and even with man, for even his ability to reproduce himself is more or less in inverse ratio to the amount of intellect, and so of food-obtaining power, he possesses. But granting all that, it may be claimed that the probable rate of increase in man, as judged by his past history, must soon bring him face to face with actual starvation for which there will be no remedy. The present rate of increase in population certainly cannot go on indefinitely on this earth. But is there not some good and wise reason for the present rapid increase, and will not this increase slow down by and by when it has accomplished its purpose? As we feel respect and reverence for the old book which taught science correctly several thousand years before man discovered it for himself, let us consult it in regard to this point. This book tells us that the Creator commanded man to be fruitful and multiply and replenish the earth *and subdue it.* Man has gone on multiplying for thousands of years, and still he is not numerous enough to fill a tenth part of the earth, and he has scarcely begun to subdue the forces of Nature to his best interests. Hundreds or thousands of years hence, when he shall have accomplished this, as we now estimate accomplishment, and the whole earth is made fertile and productive, very possibly science may have taught us so much more about the character and capacity of Nature's machine that the time of complete subjection of the earth to man's well-being may seem as far off as it now does.

The source of the most of our material resources may be traced back to the light and heat of the sun. Only an infinitesimal fraction of the sun's rays falls upon our planet, and of this but a small fraction is retained, the rest passing off by radiation. Here lies a most fascinating and fruitful field for the exercise of applied science. Could the larger part of these rays which are now lost to us be retained and used, the results would well-nigh surpass the wild dreams of the Arabian Nights' tales.*

* Since writing this it has come to my notice that a celebrated German scientist has recently suggested that the time may come

The relation between population and food supply would be made worse instead of better if the disciples of Malthus were to gain a large following, for the reason that those who would be capable of comprehending their doctrine, and who would have the character and self-control to live up to it—to sacrifice natural instincts and impulses for the good of future generations—would be the more intelligent and capable part of humanity; but this is the part which produces, directly or indirectly, by brain or muscle, more than it consumes; while the least intelligent part of humanity—that which produces less than it consumes—would still go on breeding.

The danger of this world's becoming over-burdened with human beings is certainly a very remote one, and I have no doubt that Nature will in due time make a proper adjustment between the birth-rate and the food supply without calling upon us to assist her by means degrading alike to soul and body.

---

when applied science will be able to provide food for as many human beings as would occupy this planet *if it were one vast city!*

CHAPTER VIII.

OTHER BARS TO PARENTHOOD.

ILL-HEALTH is often a good and sufficient reason why persons should not marry and become parents, but the laity are often entirely mistaken in their ideas as to the kind and degree of ill-health which is a bar to the parental relation. One may look the picture of health and imagine himself well, and yet be in a condition which will cause much trouble and sorrow after marriage, and give his descendants a right to rise up and call him anything but blessed.

On the other hand, we often see those who, to an unprofessional eye, appear delicate, even far advanced toward a fatal decline, who have nothing radically wrong with them, and who, after marriage, improve marvellously in general condition and become parents of healthy children. Some of these would probably have remained life-long invalids had they remained single; others, who improved somewhat in health, but avoided parenthood, would have enjoyed better health had they become parents.

It is not always easy nor possible to account for this, but marriage is a natural and physiological condition, and, as such, would be expected to conduce to health and vigor, though the very marked improvement which follows marriage is frequently a mystery even to the physician who carefully searches for the cause. Hereditary tendency has much to do with the matter. There are some families in which it seems to be a well-established rule that the children are delicate until marriage, and then grow robust; while in others the opposite is true. If there be no dangerous hereditary tendency, and the vital organs are in fair condition, feeble health need seldom be a bar to marriage, and if conscientious endeavor be made to that end, it may be expected that healthy, happy children will crown such a union.

Conditions vary greatly in different cases. Some have such store of vitality that the husband may devote himself assiduously to business, and the wife give much time and strength to social and other obligations, and yet their children inherit sound bodies and sunny temperaments. In other cases, the task of giving the inheritance of a good birth to one's children seems to require almost the entire vitality.

Much of the ill-health which causes respectable and well-meaning people to hesitate about undertaking the responsibilities of marriage is entirely due to petty and respectable vices, such as late hours, over-excitement, too much food with too little exercise, strong tea and coffee, tobacco, excessive use of condiments and appetizers, moderate tippling, etc., while any of these, joined to intemperance in the conjugal relation, may suffice to cause sterility, or to lay the burden of ill-health upon offspring.

Those who will be intemperate in any respect should hesitate about undertaking marriage and parenthood, and those who are anxious to have children should first seriously count the cost and see whether they are able and willing to pay it. Luxury is blamed for many of our social ills, even by people who think well of luxury. The luxury which diminishes and deteriorates a race is the abuse, not the use, of prosperity, and abuse is vice. A carriage and pair of horses, when not used for some industrial end, are a luxury, and yet may tend in many ways to the comfort, happiness, and usefulness of their possessor, so long as they are used and not misused. Many women misuse a carriage to take them everywhere they wish to go; their circulation is weak, and they are cold; their livers are sluggish, and they are tired; they misuse and over-use all their prosperity, and they are bored.

A woman who is habitually cold and tired and bored may not expect to become the mother of sound and vigorous children.

Writers often refer to the English habit of walking, especially on the part of women ; no one can understand to what an extent this is carried unless he has seen it for himself. This custom must come in vogue here if we are to have strong and healthy women among the upper classes.

The quiet and uneventful administration of President Hayes will be remembered long after some more brilliant ones have been forgotten, because his brave and queenly wife took a firm and womanly stand on the question of temperance.

Would that the present administration, which will pass into history as one of measurable success in the face of great odds, might be remembered also as the one in which the charming and sensible woman who presided at the White House had set the fashion of walking ! As the first woman of the land she may do this ; if she does, every physician in America will be her enthusiastic friend, and unborn generations will have cause to bless her name.

* * * * * *

Poverty is, perhaps, the most frequent excuse offered for unwillingness to become parents, and this often seems a sufficient reason. It is a remarkable fact that this plea is seldom used by the really poor, but frequently by those who are comparatively, or actually, well to do. There are many poor families that ought not to become larger than they are, but this is because of their vice rather than their poverty.

Poverty is one of the most difficult words to define. One feels poor because he cannot afford to give his children meat on Sundays and holidays; another, because he cannot buy his wife a silk dress and himself a gold watch; a third feels himself a poor man because he cannot live in a "brown-stone front," and a fourth because he has not $10,000 a year to spend on a yacht, and so it goes.

The most of the poverty in this world is felt by those who want what they do not need, rather than by those who cannot have what they do need. Grinding, galling poverty comes to any one whose tastes and desires are a certain distance in advance of his bank account.

The American family in comfortable circumstances usually spends about twice as much money and vitality in the rearing of children as is necessary or desirable. People assume at the outset that it will be a great expense, and for this reason frequently defer the matter of a family until they grow rich. Then they proceed to throw away money, time, and vitality in over-dressing, over-feeding, over-attending, and over-indulging their children. It would be better for them and vastly better for the children if the latter had been born earlier and received less spoiling.

A cynical wag has adapted Shakespeare to his mood and made him say: "There is a divinity which shapes our ends *rough*, hew them how we will." I believe there is a divinity which helps us to shape our ends *smooth* when we apply honest effort to those ends, be the circumstances never so unpropitious. There are countless examples of those who began married life with but a slender stock of material resources, but who bravely and cheerfully tried to meet every duty, who were prospered in every respect—in children, health, wealth, and influence. And there are as many who began with the most flattering prospects, but who from the first deliberately planned to shirk duty for selfish ends, that they might live just for themselves, who came to grief in the widest and bitterest meaning of the word.

The Creator intended that the married should become parents; He did not intend that ultimately they should gain any advantage by neglect of this duty.

* * * * * *

The discomforts and dangers of gestation are

neither few nor small; yet they are not so great in number and degree as is generally supposed, and medical science is constantly making them less. It is but a few years since she who was about to become a mother was expected to ignore her condition as far as possible. In many cases she did not feel free to discuss the matter with near female relatives and friends; shut up to herself, she became the prey of morbid fancies and horrible fears; mole-hills were magnified into mountains, and, in the case of a first pregnancy, when her ignorance was not even relieved by experience, her condition sometimes endangered reason itself.

The present state of things is much improved; the average woman knows much more about what belongs to that period than her grandmother did, and she usually feels free to seek counsel and sympathy from female friends. Another improvement which I am rejoiced to see is in the matter of "going out" during the few months preceding confinement. At this time the future mother especially needs the exercise and diversion thus obtained, and it is absurd and wicked to withhold them from her. The Germans, who, by the way, are much in advance of us in much belonging to the bearing and rearing of children, teach us a good lesson in this respect. A frequent sight on the promenade of almost any city in the German Fatherland is an officer or other person of high rank proudly escorting his wife, who is evidently soon to become a mother.

The "morning sickness" is much dreaded by some, and perhaps it will always remain more or less of a burden on the minds of those who are liable to pregnancy. Medical skill is in most cases able to mitigate this discomfort, and often altogether to cure it.

Even under the improved conditions, very many women dread the period of gestation because they are then in a morbid and distressed state of mind and body, and on this account have come to consider child-bearing a pathological process. Gestation is as truly a physiological condition as is digestion, and there is no more necessity for morbidness of mind in the one case than for dyspepsia in the other. Indeed, there is less, for Nature, who is liberal and metes out compensations with a lavish hand, has arranged that the discomforts—there must always be the disadvantage of increased weight and bulk—shall be offset by marked advantages during this period. It is difficult to obtain examples of perfectly normal gestation, because so few women are perfectly normal in mind and body ; but when they are normal or nearly so, it is a rule to which there are few exceptions that the mother-to-be is in a decidedly buoyant state of mind and in an exalted state of body and soul. I have often noticed this; so marked is it, indeed, frequently, that all the family recognize it, and rejoice when it is known that another little stranger may be expected soon; and, conversely, this is suspected when the mother is noticed to be more bright and winsome than usual.

Children born under these happy auspices are likely to be fortunate in temperament and physique, though a clean personality is a better guarantee of a good birth for one's child than is a mere state of exaltation during a few weeks or months before it is born. Our children inherit what we have been all our lives, rather than what we happen to be at the time of their birth.

The discomforts and dangers of birth-giving are considerably greater than those of the months that have gone before, but here medical science has achieved some of its most brilliant and beneficent results through the use of antiseptics and anæsthetics.

"Child-bed fever" was once the great dread and danger of this period; now it is rarely met, even in the large maternity hospitals where the conditions are most conducive to it. In the *Gebär Anstalt* at Prague the death-rate was, during the time I was there, *less than one in sixteen hundred of those delivered.*

The use of anæsthetics in midwifery is of comparatively recent date ; the results are most satisfactory ; indeed, I consider them nearly as brilliant here as in general surgery. We are under obligations to Dr. R. A. Kingman, of Boston, for his able and persistent efforts to bring this use of anæsthetics to the attention of the medical profession.* All admit that ether anæsthesia gives marked relief during labor, but some claim that it retards the natural proc-

* In an article entitled "Anæsthetics in Normal Labor" (*Boston Medical and Surgical Journal,* October 8th, 1885) Dr. Kingman says : "The subsequent effects upon the mother cannot be such as to play any important *rôle* in her convalescence ; for not being given to complete anæsthesia, its influence must be less than after even a slight surgical operation. By virtue of the rest and relief from pain afforded during labor, it ought assuredly to predispose to a more favorable convalescence. * * * With regard to the danger involved in the use of ether, the simple fact that in the nearly forty years, and among the hundreds of thousands of midwifery cases in which ether has been used, not a single death has been attributable to it, would seem to be a sufficient reply to the question. * * * As has been stated, we wish to abolish neither consciousness nor sensation, only pain. The patient is aware of the contraction, but does not suffer from it. She should be able to answer questions and carry out our directions intelligently. * * * Having at our disposal substances capable of safely and effectively relieving pain, without materially affecting the progress of labor, it becomes our duty as physicians to at least offer to our parturient patients a mitigation of their sufferings."

ess, and others that it gives rise to undesirable after effects. The former is occasionally the case; and possibly the latter is true in rare instances when complete anæsthesia is maintained for a long time. I have never met either of these objections in my own practice; indeed, my experience has been of the happiest nature. I find that *partial* anæsthesia, instead of retarding labor, decidedly assists it, and I would use it in many slow and difficult cases on this account, even though it did not afford the patient immense relief.

Anæsthesia is of great service in labor in those cases where the pains are strong enough to give the patient great distress, but still too weak to do satisfactory work. This effect of an anæsthetic probably rests more upon psychological than physiological grounds. It is well known that fright or any sudden emotion of the mind may lessen, or entirely arrest, labor pains; no doubt this, joined to the actual pain, is often the cause of dilatory or arrested labor. Anæsthesia relieves the distress of mind and body, and allows all the vitality to be used in the real work in hand, for suffering is always at the expense of vitality.* Many suppose the use of

* Labor may progress perfectly under complete anæsthesia, because the womb is controlled by muscles which are not affected by it.

ether in labor to be, in any case, difficult and dangerous. I believe the danger to be almost minimum in skilful hands, and the difficulty is so slight that I have used it with the most satisfactory results when I had no assistance except such as the patient herself could render. In such a case, of course, the point of unconsciousness is not reached. I believe complete anæsthesia to be seldom necessary, either to the improvement of the labor or the marked relief of the patient.

The time is certainly near at hand, if, indeed, it be not already come, when the discomforts and dangers of maternity need no longer deter any brave and true woman from becoming a mother.

The Prince and Princess Hohenlohe, of Austria, are a good example to those who imagine that society obligations may excuse from the duty of parenthood. They have a family of bright, healthy children. The princess has social obligations compared with which those of the average American woman are insignificant, but she considers that her children have the first right, and she punctiliously devotes one year to each child—partly before its birth and partly afterward ; it is then provided with a wet-nurse, and the princess returns to society.

CHAPTER IX.

SUGGESTIONS.

An honorable spinsterhood is a hundred times better than a dishonorable wifehood. No woman should marry unless she loves; marriage which is not a union of hearts as well as hands must always be a virtual failure. A genuine and worthy love is always founded upon respect; a love which one must first excuse, he must afterward accuse, and finally condemn.

A young woman should not forget that her lover virtually proposes himself as the future father of her children; only from this standpoint can she make an intelligent and safe estimate of him. It is a foolhardy thing for a woman to marry a man to save him, and no self-respecting man should ask it. He thereby asks her to risk her life happiness on a single throw, *and the dice are loaded.* To experienced ears a man's protestations of what he will do and be, *after marriage*, sound like the clown's wisdom—"Let not him that taketh off the armor boast like him that putteth it on." Marriage reformation is much like death-bed repentance.

> "The devil was sick,
> The devil a monk would be;
> The devil was well,
> The devil a monk was he."

A good time to learn to be a prudent, temperate, and virtuous husband and father is during the twenty years before one begins. "Cramming" sometimes enables college students to "pass" brilliant examinations, but crammed knowledge is seldom very abiding; the virtues are peculiarly difficult to "cram."

Few young women realize the power and responsibility which rest with them in the matter of checking the loose habits of young men. The latter often have the idea that they may do almost anything they please, provided they keep out of jail, and it will not seriously disturb their social position; not infrequently they boast that he who has the reputation of being a Don Juan in a small way is liked all the better! "Where there is smoke there is fire;" there is some foundation for this idea, and young women are to blame for it. The remedy is a heroic one, and only heroines can apply it.

A young woman was twice seen to decline the arm of a young man who accompanied her home from gatherings of young people. To a friend who asked the cause of this unusual proceeding she said: "I know him to be a man of impure life, and I cannot take the arm of such a man." If all had the womanliness and heroism to follow her example, the marriage and birth-rates would for a time be lowered, and the numbers of women in the ranks of the bread-winners would be correspondingly increased; but the average of virtue and the quality of posterity would be improved.

Young men should guard their virtue as a priceless treasure. Society may shut its eyes to their lapse from virtue, or may even smile at it, but society is powerless to absolve character from the damning blot. A pure, noble wife is the best gift this world holds for any man, and he can pay for it only in kind; position, wealth, and all else besides that he may offer, count but as the small dust of the balance in comparison.

So false are the ideas in regard to purity in some sections of our country that college students pretend, among themselves, to have had dishonorable experiences when their comrades know this to be untrue. It often happens that a fashion is adopted as the new and correct thing long after it has "gone out" in the locality of its birth.

This depraved fashion has, perhaps, come to us from the German university. It is beginning to "go out" there. In one of the largest and most influential of them there is a corps of students whose badge is a white cap, and whose pledge of membership is the purity of which the badge is a symbol. * * *

The idea that American girls are unwilling to begin at the beginning when they marry is, oftener than not, born of the silly pride and unworthy ambition of the men themselves. The craze for "big" things is one of the direst curses of our time and country. What we need is, not more large establishments with many servants and much ceremony, but simple, quiet *homes*, where the mad stream of daily life may rest for a little, and the domestic virtues take root; where husband and wife need not be separated by the demands of a society which regards them less for what they *are* than for what they *give;* homes in which mutual love and need shall hold the members of the matrimonial copartnership together in harmony of purpose and action which shall find its highest expression in the glad voices of merry-hearted children, who, having the rich inheritance of good birth, can never be poor, whatever the outward circumstances may be.

The highest type of American womanhood stands ready to share such homes, be they never so humble. There is no lack of girls of good family, well brought up, well educated, of unimpeachable character, and well fitted in body, mind, and heart to make happy homes, who are to be had for the asking by poor men who have sufficient character and courage to make their future reasonably sure. * * *

In this connection, just a word about the wedding dowry. Our European neighbors give it too much prominence in the matrimonial affair. We go to the other extreme, and often ignore it altogether. There is a golden mean between these extremes. It is sensible and proper—bare justice, in fact—for the man of means to give his daughter a goodly dowry at her marriage. Many a girl who marries a poor man has comparatively little, or almost nothing, at marriage, although a considerable fortune awaits her on her father's death.* There is little doubt that a sensible course in respect to the wedding dowry would save many a young couple from the sin against parenthood. * * *

It is customary for the bride-elect to spend several months or a year in special preparation for marriage. This is an excellent idea, but she should spend the time in a very different way

* Too often it is worse than nothing, for it is in the form of fine clothes and other things which, indirectly at least, lead to expense instead of being a pecuniary help to the young people, who must live on a small income.

from that which custom usually dictates. In many cases it would be well for her to dispense with a third or a half of the usual trousseau, so much of it being superfluous, and a large part of the rest should be bought ready-made, and thus an immense amount of wear and tear of her nervous system would be spared. An elaborate bridal outfit tempts to expenditure out of proportion to the means, and even when the bride-elect has little or no part in its preparation, beyond the planning and trying on of dresses and other garments, it costs her months of anxiety and exhausting work.

This time should be spent in whatever way will tend to put her into the best possible condition of mind and body, so that at marriage she may be at the acme of complete, normal womanhood. It is not easy to say just what would best accomplish this end, different cases needing different treatment; in most cases, it is probable that a course of light gymnastics, with plenty of out-door exercise, would be indicated; at the same time, any specially weak point in the physique should receive attention. A little study—enough to give zest to the exercise—will be in order also, and if she have not already done so, she should take a course in elementary physiology and hygiene. In any case, she should receive some thorough and judicious instruction especially bearing upon the new and untried world into which she is about to enter. This will often prove a delicate and difficult matter; satisfactory text-books are not to be had, and the mother, in too many cases used all her life to reticence on such subjects, may find it difficult, if not impossible, to be her instructor.

The present wedding arrangements among the well to do are calculated to adorn the young couple for society rather than to fit them for the duties and responsibilities of domestic life. The young people naturally feel that the finery is of little avail if society is not to have the benefit of it, and, not infrequently, those whose hearts prompt them to a more worthy course feel compelled to keep free from the burdens of parenthood for a season, while they meet the expectations of friends and relatives in regard to society. Years are expected to bring wisdom, and one naturally looks for more sense from parents than from their children; but it seems to me that the young couples nowadays have even more conscience and common-sense in respect to parenthood than their parents have. I oftener meet with cases where young married people wish to become parents, but are dissuaded by their parents, or where the latter are displeased because a grandchild is expected, than I do with cases where the objection to parenthood is on the part of the young people. This may not be true in all classes and in all sections of our country, but this has been my experience in my own practice. It is a good idea for the young people to go away by themselves for a few days or weeks after the wedding ceremony ; but the wedding trip, as it is too often made, is an utter abomination, and a wedding trip to Europe is the climax. The bridal pair can usually do better than to visit relatives at this time ; they can scarcely do worse than to attempt much travel and sight-seeing and the life of fashionable hotels. It is a good idea to make a short journey to some city or resort where one can find a quiet, well-conducted hotel, which furnishes every comfort and a good opportunity for the young people to be well left to themselves. Many who would prefer this sort of a wedding trip make an expensive and exhausting journey because they feel that they are expected to be able to make an impressive report on their return.

It is difficult for young married people to keep on a right basis with each other among family friends ; it is almost impossible to do so in the average boarding-house. They can keep house on what it will cost to board. It may not be quite as stylish, but it will be better in almost every way.

By the time the first few months are past, and the pair are well on the way to harmony—*not unison*—of wills as well as hearts, there are, or ought to be, family prospects. The parents-to-be properly may feel like keeping the matter to themselves for a time; society has no right to demand that they publish the fact; but if they wish credit for honesty and common sense from people who possess both, they should not in any way apologize for their condition; good sense, good taste, and good morals absolutely forbid it, and the laws of good society ought to condemn it, too.

Special effort should now be made to give the unborn child love and care. The parent may neglect it after it is born, if necessary, but may not dare to neglect it before birth. The little thing, scarcely beginning to have form or being, even in the imagination of its parents, and apparently shut away from all influence of the outside world, is yet very much under that influence, and can no more help being moved by the thousand and one pulsations of thought and feeling that touch the mother than can the centre of gravity help quivering under each footfall on the earth. The unborn child breathes the air of heaven through the mother's lungs; it sees beauty through her eyes, hears harmony through her ears; it lays up store of future gladness through her joy in all that is gladsome and good; it lays the foundation for future hope and courage through her exercise of them at this time; and its quantity and quality of brain and heart must largely depend upon the pattern she furnishes for its copying.

In view of this, will any woman dare spend these months in selfish repining or in the mad whirl of social gayety? Will any one worthy the name of *woman* dare ask for a larger or more honorable sphere than to mould the destiny of unborn generations?

* * * We hear too much about mothers being slaves to their children. This sort of slavery is less often from attention to the actual needs of the children, than from the devotion of time and vitality when they are useless, if not positively harmful. I will mention a single instance in which the mother wrongs herself and her children by ill-advised attention. This is in rocking them to sleep. Nature intended the healthy child to go to sleep by itself, and has arranged that quiet and darkness should favor sleep. Instead of this, multitudes of children are trained from earliest infancy to expect and demand to be laboriously put to sleep with the gas burning

and the mothers or nurses rocking them, and singing, or telling a bed-time story. This is bad in almost every way ; ninety-nine children out of a hundred would more quickly go to sleep without this artificial process if they had not been badly trained. The light and heat, the bed-time story, and nearly all else that belongs to the operation tend to activity of the little brains and ward off sleep. Besides this, the influence of a hurried and nervous mother or nurse is extremely bad on a delicate child. The practice of putting children to sleep is, besides, a cruelty and an injustice to the children, because it often sows the seeds of selfishness which follows them all their lives.

* * * When Nature makes a niche she furnishes an object to fill it ; when she plants the instincts of parenthood in the characters of men and women, she does not mock them with longings which may not be satisfied. Even for the few unfortunate ones who would become parents but may not, she makes provision in the unfortunate little ones whose parents have been early called away. Children sometimes seem to be born into the wrong families ; much oftener they are adopted into the wrong ones, and bitter experience has caused many to feel that adoption must always prove unsatisfactory and unsafe. There is no lack of cases, however, in

which the relation between parents and children by adoption has been in the highest degree satisfactory. Children are born rather than made, and it might be unwise to adopt a child whose birth was questionable, or worse ; but there are many orphans of good birth whose guardians would gladly give them to those who were willing and worthy to adopt them for their own. It is a pity that those who long for children should remain childless ; it is yet more a pity that children who were born into *homes* should have to be brought up—by machinery. We are justly proud of our orphan asylums. I have seen most excellent ones, but never one which was really a *home.*

There may be those who have no children of their own, and yet feel that they cannot be parents to those born of others. We may not sit in judgment on such, but they may not wash their hands of all responsibility ; directly or indirectly, childhood looks to them for love and care, and they may not honorably and safely withhold them.

Heaven speed the day when marriage shall become a holy sacrament, as the Creator intended it to be ; when maternity shall everywhere be recognized as the crown of womanhood, and when every home in our land shall contain a goodly number of children born to that best inheritance—soundness of mind and body. Then will our homes be harmonious and happy, and the State, the product of these homes, be prosperous and great. The family and the State, held together by the bond of mutual protection, shall advance onward and upward, "And a little child shall lead them."

APPENDIX.

THE PUBLIC STATUTES OF THE COMMONWEALTH OF MASSACHUSETTS.

Chapter 207.—Of Offences against Chastity, Morality, Decency, and Good Order.

SECTION 9. Whoever, with intent to procure miscarriage of a woman, unlawfully administers to her, or advises or prescribes for her, or causes to be taken by her, any poison, drug, medicine, or other noxious thing, or unlawfully uses any instrument or other means whatever with the like intent, or with like intent aids or assists therein, shall, if the woman dies in consequence thereof, be imprisoned in the State prison not exceeding twenty nor less than five years, and, if the woman does not die in consequence thereof, shall be punished by imprisonment in the State prison not exceeding seven years nor less than one year, and by a fine not exceeding two thousand dollars.

SEC. 10. Whoever knowingly advertises, prints, publishes, distributes, or circulates, or knowingly causes to be advertised, printed, published, distributed, or circulated, any pamphlet, printed paper, book, newspaper, notice, advertisement, or reference, containing words or language giving or conveying any notice, hint, or reference to any person, or to the name of any person, real or fictitious, from whom, or to any place, house, shop, or office where any person, drug, mixture, preparation, medicine, or noxious thing, or any instrument or means whatever, or any advice, direction, or information, or knowledge may be obtained for the purpose of causing or procuring the miscarriage of a woman pregnant with child, shall be punished by imprisonment in the State prison or jail not exceeding three years, or by fine not exceeding one thousand dollars. * * *

SEC. 17. Whoever sells, lends, gives away, exhibits, or offers to sell, lend, or give away an instrument or other article intended to be used for self-abuse, or any drug, medicine, instrument, or article whatever, for the prevention of conception or for causing unlawful abortion, or advertises the same, or writes, prints, or causes to be written or printed, a card, circular, book, pamphlet, advertisement, or notice of any kind stating when, where, how, or by whom, or by what means, any such article can be purchased or obtained, or manufactured, or makes any such article, shall be punished by imprisonment in the State prison for not more than five years, or in the jail or house of correction for not more than three years, or by fine of not less than one hundred nor more than one thousand dollars.

Wharton's Criminal Law, ninth edition, 1885, has the following in regard to the common law on this subject:

SEC. 592. At common law the destruction of an infant unborn is a misdemeanor, supposing the child to have been born dead, though if the child die subsequently to birth from wounds received in the womb, it is homicide, even though the child is still attached to the mother by the umbilical cord.

Destruction of the infant after quickening is agreed on all sides to be an offence at common law; though whether it is so before the infant has quickened has been doubted at common law. In determining this question we must remember that the civil rights of an infant in *rente sa mere* are equally respected at every point of gestation; and it is clear that, no matter at how early a stage, he [it] may be appointed executor; is capable of taking as legatee, or under a marriage settlement; may take specifically under a general devise as a "child;" and may obtain an injunction to stay waste.

That the destruction of an infant before quickening is a misdemeanor at common law has been held in Pennsylvania and North Carolina. A contrary view at common law has been expressed in Massachusetts, New Jersey, Iowa, Kentucky, and Missouri. * * *

SEC. 593. The woman on whom the abortion has been performed is a competent witness against the defendant, even though she be regarded as an accomplice. But in cases of force or undue influence the law regards her rather as a victim than an accomplice, though if she encouraged the attempt, this may tend to weaken the moral effect of her evidence. * * *

SEC. 594. Consent of the woman * * * is no defence. *Jus publicum privatorum voluntate nequit.*

SEC. 595. It is a defence that the destruction of the child's life was necessary to save that of the mother.

SEC. 599. All parties concerned in the offence are responsible, whatever may be the part they take, subject to the distinction heretofore laid down in respect to principals. Hence a person who receives a woman into his house for the purpose of having an abortion performed on her, and who procures a physician for the operation, is indictable for the offence as principal, if it be a misdemeanor; or, if it be a felony, and the common law distinctions obtain, as accessory before the fact, supposing he rendered no immediate aid in the operation.

SEC. 182. If the means are *apparently* adapted to the end, then the public peace, so far as the attempt is concerned, is as much disturbed as if they should be so actually ; and hence the indictment for the attempt on such evidence can be sustained. * * *

SEC. 1831. By the Revised Statutes of the United States (Sec. 3893 ; see acts March 3d, 1873 ; July 12th, 1876) it is provided "that no obscene, lewd, or lascivious book, pamphlet, picture, paper, print, or other publication of an indecent character, or any article or thing, designed or intended for the prevention of conception or procuring of abortion, nor any article or thing intended or adapted for any indecent or immoral use, nor any written or printed card, circular, book, pamphlet, advertisement, or notice of any kind, giving information, directly or indirectly, where, how, or by whom, or by what means, either of the things before mentioned may be obtained or made, * * * shall be carried in the mail, and any person who shall knowingly deposit. or cause to be deposited, for mailing or delivery, any of the hereinbefore-mentioned articles or things, etc., * * * shall be deemed guilty of misdemeanor," etc.

It will be noticed that the common law regards the prevention of conception as a crime, inasmuch as it punishes the furnishing or advertising of means for it.

The distinction between an infant before and after "quickening" is not justly made. No infant is "viable" at the age when "quickening" usually occurs; and, on the other hand, quickening may not occur at all, and yet the infant be in a normal condition, be born alive, and live.

I am indebted to the custodian of the Law Library at the Boston Court House for the privilege of examining the laws of all the States and Territories, and for many courtesies extended to me during my somewhat long and tedious researches there. I give a tabulated statement of the gist of such laws as specially bear upon my subject, as far as I was able to find any. The statutes, digests, etc., of the States and Territories, as found in this library, fill more than eight hundred volumes, some of which are the size of a Webster's "Unabridged." I was obliged to search a large part of these. As the different States have different methods of arrangement and indexing, some of them very imperfect, and as I am not at home in a law library, I have not been able to do the work with as great accuracy as I could wish. It is possible that in some cases there may be later and more stringent laws than those I have found, or laws in some of the States and Territories in which I found none, though as regards the latter I believe I in every case found the chapter in which such laws would naturally appear, and read it carefully.

It will be noticed that Kentucky, New Jersey, Oregon, South Carolina, Texas, and the District of Columbia are the only places in which I have failed to find some local law against abortion.

Eight States and Territories—viz., California, Connecticut, Dakota, Indiana, New Hampshire, New York, Wisconsin, and Wyoming, punish the woman upon whom the abortion is attempted.

Eight States—viz., California, Indiana, Kansas, Massachusetts, Michigan, Nebraska, New York, and Ohio, punish the advertising or furnishing of means for the prevention of conception; and Ohio makes it a crime to even have such means in one's possession.

Three States—viz., Illinois, Indiana, and Michigan, have strict laws against advertising or selling medicines especially for female use; such as have a "caution to the married," are described in ambiguous language, etc.

In nearly every instance the "attempt to procure" is made as comprehensive as possible; and in many instances it is specified that it makes no difference that pregnancy did not actually exist, nor that the means used could not have accomplished the end sought.

Nearly every State and Territory has strict laws for punishing the concealment of the birth of a child which, if born alive, would have been illegitimate, so that it may not be known whether such child was not, in fact, born alive and murdered.

In every instance there is an exception made in favor of those cases in which the early birth of the infant is necessary to save the life of the mother.

STATE.	In Case of Death of Mother or Child.	Attempt to Perform Abortion.	Punishment of the Woman.	Advertising or Selling Means for Abortion.	Advertising or Selling Means for Prevention of Conception.	Remarks.
Alabama.		— $500 and may be 3–12 mo. imp.				
Arizona.		2–5 y. imp.				
Arkansas.		— $1000 and 1–5 y. imp.		$1000 and 6–12 mo. imp.		Destruction of "quick" child manslaughter, 1874; other law, 1884.
California		2–5 y. imp.	1–5 y. imp.	Felony.	Felony.	
Colorado.	Manslaughter (if woman die).	— $1000 and — 3 y. imp.				
Conn.		— $1000 or — 5 y. imp. or both.	— $500 or — 2 y. imp. or both.	— $500.		
Dakota.	4 — y. imp.		— $1000 or — 1 y. imp. or both.			
Delaware.		$100–$500 and 1–5 y. imp.		$50–$200 and — 1 y. imp.		Law made in 1883.
Florida.	Manslaughter 2d degree, in case of "quick" child.	— $1000 or 1–7 y. imp.		— $1000 or — 1 y. imp.		

State.	In Case of Death of Mother or Child.	Attempt to Perform Abortion.	Punishment of the Woman.	Advertising or Selling Means for Abortion.	Advertising or Selling Means for Prevention of Conception.	Remarks.
Georgia.		— $1000 or — 12 mo. imp. or both.				
Idaho.		2–5 y. imp.				
Illinois.	Murder.	1–10 y. imp.		$50–$500* or 3 d.–6 mo. imp.		Law strict about selling medicines for females exclusively.
Indiana.	$50–$500 and 3–14 y. imp.	$10–$500 and 30 d.–12 mo. imp.	$10–$500 and 30 d.–12mo. imp.	$5–$500, and may add 10 d.–6 mo. imp.	$5–$500, and may add 10 d.–6 mo. imp.	Includes medicines sold or advertised with caution to the married.
Iowa.		— $1000 and — 1 y. imp.				
Kansas.		Manslaughter 2d degree, of "quick" child.		$50–$1000 or 30 d.–6 mo. imp. or both.	$50–$1000 or 30 d.–6 mo. imp. or both.	
Kentucky						
Louisiana		1–10 y. imp.				
Maine.	If child die — $1000 or — 5 y. imp.	— $1000 and — 1 y. imp.				

Maryland.		$500–$1000 or 3 — y. imp. or both.		$500–$1000 or 3 — y. imp. or both.		
Mass.	If the woman die, 5–20 y. imp.	— $2000 and 1–7 y. imp.		— $1000 or — 3 y. imp.	$100–$1000 or — 5 y. imp.	
Michigan.	Manslaughter.	— $500 or — 1 y. imp or both.		$50–$100† or — 3 mo. imp. or both.	$50–$100 or — 3 mo. imp. or both.	Heavy fine for advertising medicines in ambiguous language.
Miss.		Manslaughter in case of "quick" child.				
Missouri.	Manslaughter 2d degree, if woman die.	— $500 or — 1 y. imp. or both.				
Montana.		2–5 y. imp.				
Nebraska.		— $500 or — 1 y. imp. or both.		— $1000 or — 6 mo. imp. or both.	— $1000 or — 6 mo. imp. or both.	
Nevada.		1–10 y. imp.		1–10 y. imp.		
N. H.	Murder 2d degree, if woman die.	— $1000 or — 1 y. imp. or both.	— $1000 or 1 y. imp. or both.			Attempted abortion of "quick" child — $1000 and 1–10 y. imp.

* For selling; advertising is — 3 years' imprisonment or — $1000.
† May be sold on prescription of regular physician, but the seller must keep full record of transaction.

STATE.	In Case of Death of Mother or Child.	Attempt to Perform Abortion.	Punishment of the Woman.	Advertising or Selling Means for Abortion.	Advertising or Selling Means for Prevention of Conception.	Remarks.
New Mex.	Murder 3d degree, if woman die.					Attempted abortion of "quick" child murder, 3d degree.
N. Jersey.						
N. York.	5–20 y. imp. if woman die.	— 4 y. imp.	In case of "quick" child, — $1000* or 1–15 y. imp. or both.	Advertising, misdemeanor; furnishing, felony.	— $500 or — 1 y. imp. or both.	Destruction of "quick" child 5–20 y. imp.
N. C.		Felony or misdemeanor.				
Ohio.	If woman die 1–7 y. imp.	If successful 1–7 y. imp.		— $1000 or — 6 mo. imp. or both.	— $1000 or — 6 mo. imp. or both.	Possession of means for abortion or prevention of conception $50–$1000 or — 1 y. imp. or both.
Oregon.						
Penn.	— $500 and — 7 y. imp.	— $500 and — 3 y. imp.				Ambiguous use of "quick."
Rhode I.	If woman die 5–20 y. imp.	1–7 y. imp.		— 3 y. imp.		

S. C.						
Tenn.	1–5 y. imp.	1–3 y. imp.				
Texas.						
Utah.		2–10 y. imp.				
Vermont.	If woman die 5–20 y. imp.	3–10 y. imp.		$200–$500 and 1–3 y. imp. for furnishing.		Advertising means for abortion 3–10 y. imp.
Virginia.	If child die 3–5 y. imp.	If successful 3–5 y. imp.		$100–$500 and 1–12 mo. imp.		
Wash. T.	1–20 y. imp.	1–5 y. imp. or — $1000 and 1–12 mo. imp.				
West Va.		If successful 1–5 y. imp.				
Wisconsin	4–7 y. imp.	$250–$500 or 6 mo.–1 y. imp. or both.	— $100 or 1–6 mo. imp.			
Wy. T.	— $1000 and 3 — y. imp.	— $1000 and 3 — y. imp.	In case of illegitimate child — 1 y. imp.			
Dist. of C.						

* Otherwise 1–4 years.